The Meaning of Faith and Mental Illness

Greg Denniston

Bloomington, IN Milton Keynes, UK

authorHOUSE™

AuthorHouse™
1663 Liberty Drive, Suite 200
Bloomington, IN 47403
www.authorhouse.com
Phone: 1-800-839-8640

AuthorHouse™ UK Ltd.
500 Avebury Boulevard
Central Milton Keynes, MK9 2BE
www.authorhouse.co.uk
Phone: 08001974150

First published by AuthorHouse 5/17/2006

ISBN: 1-4259-0009-7 (sc)

Library of Congress Control Number: 2006904742

Printed in the United States of America
Bloomington, Indiana

This book is printed on acid-free paper.

Table of Contents

ACKNOWLEDGEMENTS i

PREFACE...v

INTRODUCTION...vii

CHAPTER 1 HOW I GOT HERE 1

CHAPTER 2 WHAT'S IN A NAME? 20

CHAPTER 3 MEANING LOST 33

CHAPTER 4 ON HOLY GROUND 52

CHAPTER 5 JESUS: LIKE US, ONLY MORE 75

GLOSSARY...97

APPENDIX 109

BIBLIOGRAPHY... 111

ACKNOWLEDGEMENTS

This book could not have been written were it not for the support of many friends. Several friends from various disciplines took this book seriously enough to honor me with their constitutive criticisms. Their input, suggestions, clarifications and queries have strengthened this work immeasurably. Feedback and support from my friends have coalesced in ways that encouraged me to begin, sustain and complete the book.

I am grateful to the many consumers I have worked with as clients. Although anonymous, these brave souls have been my greatest teachers as I have struggled to become a clinician. Thanks also goes to the consumers who have been and remain friends and peers in recovery. All of you have taught me so much about myself, about recovery, about ministry and about clinical commitment and integrity. It needs to be said that my personal and professional relationships with other consumers have shaped deeply the contours and themes of this book.

I have to thank my employer, the Adult and Child Center in Indianapolis, Indiana, for allowing me to conceive and facilitate my Spiritual Skills in Recovery Group. This Christmas marks three years that the Group has met on a weekly basis. Without Adult and Child's support and approval I would not have had the opportunity to do group therapy from a psychospiritual perspective. I am fortunate to be employed by such a progressive, forward-thinking provider of mental health services. After all, how many mental health centers are there that have allowed openly public consumers the opportunity to offer group therapy from a spiritual point of view? Not many I should think.

In that regard, I must say thanks to the clients and peers who have attended this Group. My client-peers have allowed me to put into clinical practice many of the ideas that are part of this book. I thank you one and all who have helped shape this book by your willingness to abide and engage with my unorthodox interventions. Thanks for your love, faith, support and willingness to take seriously my eccentricities, vagaries and musings. Your commitment to our Group has helped give birth to this book. Thank you.

Also, I have been blessed these many years by my Mom and Dad, Bob and Dot Denniston. I am certain I could not have sustained 14 years of recovery without your patient love and support. My parents have been some of the biggest cheerleaders for me to begin, sustain and complete this work. They were always available to provide supportive feedback from their perspective as parents of a child who has severe mental illness. They, too, have read the manuscripts and provided many excellent critiques that strengthened the presentation of the ideas of this piece.

Yet, the position of honor goes to my wife, Cindy. Without Cindy this book would never have come to be. For it was she who first urged, cajoled and demanded that I write it. She gave me courage to begin this endeavor. She had faith in me and in the need for this effort long before I ever began my initial scribbling. Cindy has been my partner from beginning to end. She alone has suffered with me throughout the entire process of writing and rewriting. When I was afraid she gave me hope to write and dream. When I was obsessive and overdrawn she helped me to stop, rest, eat and sleep. When I needed to clarify ideas she would stay awake with me long hours into the night. She never faltered in being present and available to listen to ideas, to suggest revisions and to provide much-needed perspective. When I despaired of ever finishing Cindy's gentle encouragement gave me rest and resolve. When I was grandiose she kept me planted on solid earth.

It is to Cindy Denniston that this book is dedicated.

Greg Denniston
Christmas 2005

PREFACE

This is a book about mental illness. This is a book about faith. Taken together, this book is about the psychospiritual unity of human being that finds expression in human being's primary character as a maker of meaning. As such, this book can be read as one consumer's attempt to come to terms with his experience of severe mental illness. It can also be read as a small contribution to the emerging perspectives that construct theology from the locale of disability. In this case, theology is rendered from the vantage of the disabling realities of neurochemical disease.

Although this book can be regarded somewhat as an essay in pastoral or practical theology influenced by process thought, my hope is that this little piece can benefit several audiences. It is written in hope that students of religion, seminarians, theologians and pastoral care givers will find it to be a personal and professional resource. It is written in hope that students of behavioral health care and mental health professionals can learn from it and use it as a clinical resource. It is written in hope that family members who have loved ones with mental illness can come to understand better some of the psychospiritual dilemmas faced by consumers. In all these ways, it is written in hope that consumers will find greater empowerment and hope in our experiences of recovery.

Chapter 1 is thus somewhat an autobiographical account of the psychospiritual experiences that are foundational for this book. Chapter 2 defines meaning making as the essence or primary character of human being and human activity. Chapter 3 outlines the pathologies that inhibit meaning making. Chapter 4 portrays certain elements of the Bible's fascination with psychospiritual anomalies. Chapter 5 develops a clinical theodicy based on my readings of the psychospiritual experiences of Jesus.

INTRODUCTION

I have often said that if I had to choose a time and place in history to have mental illness it would be now, here in North America. There are many reasons I feel this way. The biggest reason has to do with the proliferation and recent development of more effective and healthier treatments for severe mental illness.

Let me start my explanation with improvement in the negatives, in other words, the bad things that don't happen to us anymore. We-- people with severe mental illnesses--are no longer "warehoused" in the old psychiatric hospital system. We are no longer lobotomized. We are no longer burned at the stake. We are no longer whisked away from our homes on "ships of fools." We are no longer caged or bound by ball and chain. We are no longer treated by insulin shock to treat our psychoses. We are no longer "reposed" with cold water bath treatments. We haven't been exterminated or used as guinea pigs in concentration camps since WW II. I thank God with utmost sincerity that I have not been so unfortunate as to be victimized by these failed efforts at "treatment."

Now, let me say a few words about the positive advances in treatment. Better, more effective medications are making recovery a greater likelihood for more of us. In fact, it was the discovery of first-generation medications like thorazine and stellazine that helped drive the great exodus begun in the 1950's from the old psych hospitals back into our communities. Just in the past 15 years advances in pharmacological science have produced the atypical class of antipsychotics, the SSRI antidepressants, and even newer anti-depressants that go beyond the SSRI's. I cannot say enough about how these newer medications have made life more palatable for so many of us. I thank God with utmost sincerity that my life's meaning and satisfaction have been enhanced by such newer medications. I thank God that pioneering researchers in medical science and the pharmaceutical industry labor to develop such beneficial medical advances.

However, even these modern "wonder drugs" are not without deficits. We are learning that there can be gross weight gain associated with these newer medications. We are learning that some newer medications can increase or decrease normal, healthy levels of hormonal systems. For instance, some of us have suffered with the sexual dysfunctions and hormonal imbalances associated with increased levels of prolactin that can exist as side effects. Others of us face an increased risk and development of diabetes and/or increased cholesterol levels--which singly, or in tandem, can increase our potential for later coronary disease. There is in fact a plethora of side effects that can diminish some of the benefits and/or effectiveness of the new medications.

Nevertheless, I remain optimistic and place much hope in medical science. So, even though the present is the best time (so far) to have severe mental illness, the future will almost certainly be even better. For already pharmacological science is working to decrease, minimize, and even eradicate such unforeseen, yet debilitating side effects. Not only that, but medical science is seeking advances in pharmacology that will target many current problem areas.

For instance, significant cognitive deficits and impairments can further disable many persons with severe mental illness. I know for a fact that pharmaceutical companies like Eli Lilly and Co. here in Indianapolis, Indiana, are hard at work to find medications that increase cognitive functioning. We know that consumers smoke tobacco at higher percentages than the general population. Now we know why. Nicotine can actually help calm and sedate the anxiety and some positive symptoms of severe mental illness; for medical science has proven that some, if not many psych medications' efficacy can be enhanced by nicotine. Thus, again, I know for a fact that pharmaceuticals are researching how to engineer and deliver nicotine, or similar agents, to the brain without the damaging side-effects of smoking and addiction. Efforts are also underway to find psychiatric medications that do not carry any increase in weight-again associated with their use and administration. There is indeed a proliferation of research projects being done to improve our medications, to make them safer and more healthful. I hope that in 50 years or so further advances in psych medications will render today's "miracles" as "yesterday's barbarisms." I pray to God with utmost sincerity that this will be so.

Other advances in treatment modalities have made and are making life better for consumers. There are several "evidence-based practices" that carry empirical validation of being therapeutically effective. For instance, Assertive Community Treatment teams (ACT) are revolutionizing community-based standards of treatment for mental illness. Developed in the 1970's in Wisconsin, ACT teams have successfully kept more consumers in our homes, in our communities, out of jail and prison, and out of the hospitals--more than any other mental health treatment or delivery system has yet. In brief, ACT teams do not rely on consumers coming to the mental health centers to receive traditional treatments. Rather, ACT teams aggressively provide treatments such as case management, meds management, help with activities of daily living, entitlement and budget assistance, supported employment, among others in the homes of consumers. For an in-depth discussion of the ACT model, I refer the interested reader to this book, written by Deborah Allness and William H. Knoedler, *The PACT Model.* Other "evidence-based practices" include IDDT (Integrated Dual Diagnosis Treatment) and IMR (Illness Management and Recovery), along with others. I thank God with utmost sincerity for such advances in treatment delivery systems.

I also believe that advocacy movements have made and are helping to make these to be the "best of times" (so far) to have severe mental illness. For instance, one such grassroots group is the National Alliance on Mental Illness, or NAMI. NAMI has state and local affiliates in each of our 50 states, with a membership approaching 250,000 people. Comprised mostly of family members who have loved ones with mental illness, NAMI also attracts many consumers to its ranks. At the national level, NAMI has advocated in Congress and in State Legislatures to achieve federal and state standards that mandate parity in health insurance for persons who suffer with severe mental illness. Prior to parity, any insurance company could legally refuse to extend health care benefits to any person who had a diagnosis of mental illness. NAMI has also advocated at state and federal levels to ensure adequate coverage and reforms in Medicaid, Medicare and Social Security entitlements for persons with mental illness. NAMI is a staunch supporter of efforts to increase the prevalence and implementation of ACT teams and other evidence-based practices. NAMI has fought hard at federal, state and local levels to ensure more adequately that consumers have economic access to the newer psych medications that are so extremely expensive.

NAMI also provides group supports for families and consumers in local affiliates, to provide "safe space" for persons to share in community the emotional burdens of mental illness. NAMI offers many excellent educational programs to help families understand severe mental illness better and thereby help their afflicted loved ones; programs for consumers taught by fellow consumers to learn to manage our illnesses; programs for mental health professionals taught by teams comprised of providers, family members and consumers; and programs for clergy, police and corrections personnel. These are only some of NAMI's many successful and influential advocacy, educational and support services.

Another leader and stakeholder in the advocacy movement is the Mental Health Association, or MHA. The MHA, like NAMI, is involved in legislative, educational and support programs to benefit consumers, providers and families at local, state and national levels. Also, consumers are finding our own "voices" by banding together to develop our own advocacy groups. As a result of all these movements, once disparate groups have found common cause as stakeholders, cooperating together in dialogue to impact treatment issues, access to meds, legal standards in a variety of problems, policy formation, and clergy. I thank God with utmost sincerity for the growth of and contributions these stakeholders make in the lives of consumers, families and the public.

Even though there is obviously much progress to celebrate, problems remain. Thus, the particular problem this book seeks to address is that of bringing together consumers, mental health professionals, and clergy/faith groups. Let me explain the problem by reference to myself as an example or case of the problem. I am a person who suffers with symptoms of severe mental illness, albeit in recovery for 14 years now. I am a consumer who must receive medical, mental health treatment services to remain in and sustain my recovery. I am a person of faith and spiritual quest who seeks value and understanding to enhance my recovery. These are the three horizons I inhabit that shape my experience of life's meaning: personal mental illness, an ongoing need for mental health treatment, and an interest in things spiritual and theological. I inhabit these horizons professionally as well. I am a consumer provider. I am a mental health professional and student who is keenly interested in topics of psychology and trends in mental health treatment. I am also a minister trained as a mental health chaplain who is engaged in and energized by theological studies. The problem, for many other consumers and myself, is that more often than not these three horizons rarely fuse together in cooperation and mutual understanding. Instead, these three horizons are often at odds with each other.

Let me start with a fairly typical experience of mental illness. Often enough, symptoms of severe mental illness will include religious obsessions, delusions and/or fears that are extremely ingrained and pervasive. When some of our symptoms with religious features are disclosed to providers, many clinicians immediately dismiss such religiously oriented fascinations as being pure pathology. For historically, many mental health professionals have been all too eager to discredit any expressions of religious value or sentiment. Part of this clinical problem derives from the unfortunate historical fact that most clinicians have been trained to avoid dealing with clients' faith-based and spiritual problems. Thus, the tendency of formal training has been to refer spiritual matters to pastors or pastoral care givers. Even when our symptoms are being managed and subdued, the historical tendency of psychology, based on Freud, has been to dismiss the value of faith or spirituality in recovery processes for consumers and families. Unfortunately, such providers have been taught to see only "bad faith" or pathology in even healthy expressions of faith or spirituality.

I know this as a personal and professional fact. Some of the people who have treated me have been critical, dismissive and/or hostile to my interest in matters of faith, spirituality, and Christian theology. Most consumers I have had as friends or clients have shared with me similar rebuffs to their statements or concerns of faith by (some of) their treatment team members. Even when our faith or spirituality have not been discredited or ignored by our clinicians, most of our requests for help to resolve our crises of faith are turned away. This is because the overwhelming majority of mental health professionals have no training or personal experience to undertake the daunting task of reconstructing the soul and healing the psychological wounds and disintegrative losses that accompany the experience of severe mental illness. Thus, our existential pain and distress wrought by ruptures in psychospiritual health are left untreated and tend to remain as open, unhealed wounds. For most mental health professionals sometimes do not understand and thereby cannot treat crises of faith. Again, this is due to a historical lack of sufficient theological, pastoral or spiritual training and expertise to begin and sustain the process of helping us to heal the psychospiritual losses and destruction that are part of our experiences with catastrophic illness. Or, prejudice has rendered faith itself as an obstacle to recovery, for example as portrayed in and by Freudian traditions.

Even as my faith has been ill-respected by some providers, my symptoms, experiences, ongoing need for medication and psychological treatment have been poorly understood by many Christians I have known. As I have faced theological and faith-based ostracism, such is the case for many consumers. Problematics in faith communities are pandemic and meaningful care is rare when it comes to supporting, understanding and ministering to the psychological and psychiatric distress that we and our families face.

For instance, when "chronically normal" parishioners have cancer, surgery, or chronic health problems that require hospitalization, church members tend to kick into supportive "high gear." Sick parishioners tend to be inundated by supportive phone calls, hospital visits by the pastor and friends, and surpluses of "get well" cards. Often times ill parishioners even receive dinners prepared by the "ladies' auxiliary" during convalescence. But those of us with mental illness and our families rarely receive any of these sorts of encouraging supports from our church communities. Most pastors and parishioners are intimidated, threatened, and frightened by persons who have mental illness and are loath to visit us either at home or during our hospital stays. Neither do we or our families receive many "get well" cards when we are symptomatic. I have yet to blessed as a recipient of parish-catered dinners after being hospitalized; and I have yet to meet a consumer or family who has. This is not to say that there are not churches and church folk who do provide such wonderful support, it's only that such blessings have not been part of my realm of experience.

Most pastors are ill prepared to deal with the crises of severe mental illness that some of their church members face. Even though it is estimated that 40% of consumers and families contact their pastors first when mental illness strikes, many pastors lack even sufficient knowledge and skill to know how, when and to whom to make appropriate referrals for mental health treatment. Moreover, it is regrettably true that very few parish ministers possess sufficient interest, training, or experience to provide substantive and durative pastoral counseling to afflicted consumers and our families.

Accordingly, most consumers with severe mental illness avoid active attendance at or participation in congregational life and worship. One problem is that the income of many consumers is at poverty levels such that we are reluctant to attend worship in "unsuitable" clothes that have been obtained possibly from the Goodwill store or other thrift shops. After all, most parishioners attend churches where their "Sunday-best" clothes are the norm. Another problem is that many parishes and pastors simply don't know how to help us when we are having problems or are symptomatic. For most "chronically normal" clergy and church-goers just don't want to see persons with schizophrenia walking around the sanctuary while talking to their "voices," or stepping outside frequently to smoke during worship hour. Yet, there are hopeful examples of urban parishes that have done just that by opening their doors to welcome homeless persons who often have untreated severe mental illness. Nevertheless, some consumers with depression report that they are marginalized by pastor and parish for exhibiting too much "doom and gloom." After all, depressive symptoms spoil the high-octane "feel goodism" that many churches like to project to attract vibrant new members.

There are even severe problems amongst many pastoral counselors and hospital chaplains when it comes to ministering with impaired consumers and our families. I am personally and professionally aware that many pastoral counselors actually refuse to take on as clients persons who suffer with severe mental illness. First, most consumers cannot afford to pay for pastoral counseling, as fees are usually set too high for us and are affordable only to middle and upper class individuals. Second, few pastoral counselors elect to take on clients with severe mental illness because we are regarded as being unable to engage in the sorts of "insight" therapies that remain current in pastoral counseling circles. Third, even when we are taken on as clients, trends in pastoral counseling continue to rely on and emphasize "family systems" and/or psychodynamic theories and treatment modalities that end up blaming us and/or our families for being the very cause of our own mental illnesses. Thus, the overwhelming domain of clients acceptable for pastoral counseling is the "walking wounded" and the "worried well."

When it comes to the availability of appropriately trained and interested hospital chaplains, the forecast for meaningful care and ministry with consumers is dismal. For very few hospital chaplains opt to specialize in mental health chaplaincy during their periods of post-graduate clinical training. For it is more lucrative and marketable to specialize in oncology, pediatric care, trauma, surgical care, or intensive care than to seek to become a mental health chaplain. Face it, the employment demand for mental health chaplains has decreased markedly since de-institutionalization has emptied most psychiatric hospitals. There is simply very little demand for trained mental health clergy. Demand issues get worse when we consider that very few tertiary hospitals seek to employ mental health chaplains, as fewer and fewer hospital systems are offering inpatient care and treatment for persons with severe mental illness. For, once more, inpatient psychiatric care is not lucrative or profitable, as such care is one of, if not the most expensive of health care services for hospitals to provide.

With respect to the curricula that pastoral counselors are exposed to, I hold the seminaries accountable for being uninformed. For when it comes to being aware of and teaching cutting edge mental health treatments and services, I find the seminaries to be in the "Dark Ages." It is my contention that even the best and most progressive of liberal and mainline seminaries teach precious little about rehabilitative psychology, neurochemistry, neuropathology, supportive employment, supportive education, evidenced-based practices, ACT models and community-based treatment, or even the basics of meds management and psychopharmacology. Not only are these curricula deficits distressing, but they are also quite ironic. For the best, most progressive and liberal of America's seminaries pride themselves on their historically proven track records and abilities to provide theological education that is on the cutting edge of cultural developments and movements. Yet, I see little that the mainline and liberal seminaries have to be proud of when it comes to dealing with the evils and difficult issues of severe mental illness.

Likewise, I find little to celebrate with respect to the teachings of conservative seminaries and the practices of conservative churches. I am aware of two extremes. On the one hand there are conservative seminaries and churches that regard themselves as "progressive" in their curricula and practice. Such groups tend to rely on family systems and psychodynamics, which places them squarely in the "Dark Ages" regarding treatment options for severe mental illness. On the other hand, there are the conservative seminaries and churches that produce and employ the so-called "Christian Counselors." As I understand this latter movement, such practitioners regard sin as being the primary cause of mental illness. Hence, their cure resides in the afflicted person's ability to "get right" with God. Either way, the impact of the teachings and practices of the conservative seminaries and churches end up blaming consumers and/or our families for causing our mental illnesses. Via the "progressive" employment of family systems and psychodynamics, our families are blamed for making us their "identified patients" as the result of family dysfunction and stress. Or, consumers end up being regarded as having character flaws or weak coping systems which render us as having mental illness. Via the "Christian Counselors" it is assumed that we have chosen to live in sin apart from God's precepts and thus will suffer with symptoms of mental illness until we "get right" with God.

As I understand the basic dynamics of this phenomenon, "getting right" with God is ultimately an act of faith and contrition. The cause and personal experience of severe mental illness are thus issues of faith and sin. We are told by conservative preachers or "Christian Counselors" that if we had enough faith (usually the faith of a mustard seed, or faith to move mountains) we could be healed of our infirmities by "getting right" with God. If we truly have faith, we will be cured as a matter of course. If we lack sufficient faith to "believe God for the miracle," we remain in a state of unforgiven sin and cannot be cured, as a matter of course. I have had many friends and clients who have succumbed to such simplistic gymnastics.

However, I am aware of loving and compassionate conservative congregations and persons who are very accepting and supportive of their parishioners who have severe mental illness. I have some consumer friends who attend conservative churches where they feel honored, respected and supported, without being victimized by efforts to have them "get right" with God. Such congregations and persons have learned to understand that "getting right with God" can very much include consumers' needs for medication to "restore our souls." The caveat that I myself have experienced is that within my (conservative) denomination, I have received most of my support from ministers, teachers, families and parishioners who have had to face severe mental illness themselves in one form or another.

Nevertheless, in the pews sits a consumer who has returned to his/her "right mind" with effective treatment and medication management. S/He thus feels secure and healthy. However, the preacher stipulates with unquestionable authority that true faith in God can heal any disease, illness or infirmity. In fact, the preacher declares further that medical treatment and interventions are human solutions and are thus only a partial fix or crutch. Instead, true faith and obedience in God are the ultimate solution and cure for illness. True faith, we are told, can cure us permanently and thereby "deliver" us from taking and relying on (those crutches) medications.

S/He goes home from church feeling "convicted" by the preacher's authoritative words (held to be inspired directly by God and the Holy Spirit) that our reliance on medication is a sign of weakness, reliance on an ungodly crutch, or ultimately sinful rebellion against God. The divine solution, s/he thinks is merely to trust God in faith, again the faith of a mustard seed to move mountains, by casting away our crutch- -our psych medications. This act of obedient faith will enable us to "get right" with God. So, as a person of true faith, we "sell out" to God's Holy Spirit "without compromise" when we stop taking our prescribed medications to prove our faithful worth. Yet, as s/he always learns, in one to two weeks without medication, our acts of faith to "get right" with God have led to a relapse of our symptoms of severe mental illness. A crisis of faith and medical catastrophe ensues.

As such indisputable "truths" or "thoughts of faith" are severely reinforced and ingrained, we reason that we remain disobedient sinners, who lack enough faith to be cured, although we have cast away our medications in hope and trust. If we resume taking our prescribed medication, we feel guilty and ashamed because we don't have enough faith to move that "mountain of illness." But when we "believe God" for a healing cure by stopping our medication, we end up, once again, being dreadful sinners--for without our medication the symptoms of severe mental illness return with renewed vigor and quite often with increased impairment. For the very presence of a return of symptoms means our faith was lacking to heal us--sinners we were, sinners we remain...sinners with disabling symptoms of severe mental illness. So much for "getting right" with God.

The problem for consumers is obviously catastrophic. But I have only scratched the surface. This is because the dynamics of the inter-actions between the personal experience of severe mental illness, one's integrity and character of faith, and the need for medical treatment are highly problematic and complex.

Thus, I hazard that consumers actually have a right to fear the mental health establishment. For historically, such persons had us "ware-housed," lobotomized, caged, bound with shackles, ball and chain, etc.; and many providers have held our faith in contempt. I hazard that consumers have a right to fear and mistrust of churches and faith groups. For historically, these are the folks who brought us the Inquisition, who tortured and burned us at the stake as witches; and who call us sinners with "little faith" as they blame us for not being able to "get right" with God. Even the liberals can be indicted for their reliance on psychody-namics and family systems that blame us and/or our families for our having mental illness. I hazard that mental health professionals have a right to fear and mistrust faith communities. For these caretakers have often been "left to pick up the pieces" of our souls that have been damaged by repeated failures of not being able to "get right" with God.

I hazard that faith communities have a right to be suspicious of the mental health establishment. For there have been traditions in social work, psychology, and psychiatry which take pride in their movements as being secular alternatives and challenges to an all-too smug, orthodox tradition of bankrupt and defective Christian faith. I hazard that both faith communities and the mental health establishments have a right to fear consumers. For when we are untreated or are symptomatic, we are at best odd and eccentric, let alone when at worst, we can be dangerous to ourselves, others and/or property.

Well, this little book is one small effort, written by one hopeful consumer, to try to begin to address and resolve these and other problems that involve the confluence of mental illness, issues of faith, and issues of treatment. Yet, I am hopeful. For the contents of this book have been faithfully fashioned and pragmatically tested. I have been privileged to use the ideas and sentiments of this book as interventions and treatments with consumers and family members. In these ways, such sentiments have been warmly and well received for the most part by most of my clients and friends. With consumers, I have used these ideas in inpatient and outpatient settings, in individual counseling and group therapy. However, I caution that these interventions have been employed with people who have been on medication and who have some degree of insight, receptivity, and stability. Hence, I have little experience of offering these notions to souls who have been untreated and have been symptomatically resistant to treatment. With families and providers, I have shared these ideas both personally and professionally. I hope, then, that consumers, family members, clergy, faith groups, and mental health professionals will be able to employ this book's peculiar and particular sentiments to help empower and heal us, as we struggle together in the quest for sanity. Thus, I offer this little book to consumers, families, faith groups, and mental health professionals in the hope that it might inspire all of us to dialogue, to learn from one another, and to help us deal with the problems wrought by severe mental illness. Perhaps through mutual exchange we--all of us-- can learn to employ faith and spiritual sentiment as resources for initial and sustained recovery.

When they came up out of the water, the Spirit of the Lord snatched Philip away; the eunuch saw him no more...But Philip found himself at Azotus. Acts 8:39-40

Chapter 1
How I Got Here

In 1985, I had successfully completed my first year of studies towards a Master's degree in religion, on a full-tuition scholarship at the Iliff School of Theology in Denver, Colorado. At that time I was snatched away from reality by the onset of severe mental illness. "Snatched" is probably not severe enough a term to describe the traumas of the onset of mental illness, but it will suffice. I was 23 years old; and fortunately, the onset of my illness was a bit later in life than for many persons who share my diagnosis of schizoaffective disorder. This meant I had accumulated some successes in life and had accomplished some important developmental tasks that would aid in my recovery. However, many persons with severe mental illnesses get snatched away from reality in their late teens and accordingly lose out on a lot of major developmental experiences that consequently make their recovery harder.

1

Prior to being snatched from reality, I had a life. All my life I had been successful at academics and athletics--throughout grade school, junior high school and high school. High school included several successes. I was class president my junior year. My senior year I was vice-president of my class. I was a starting member of a top-ten rated basketball team in the state of Indiana. I was a Rotary Club Sportsmanship Award winner. I was charter president of the Mayor's City Youth Commission in my hometown. I graduated from high school with a 3.5 GPA and was voted Outstanding Senior Male by our graduating class. It should be of no surprise that I was pretty cocky. That was 1980.

By 1984, I had graduated from Anderson College, a liberal arts school in my home town. I graduated *cum laude* with a 3.84 GPA with majors in Philosophy and Religion. I had managed to work an average of 25-30 hours per week as I put myself through college. I got married after the first semester of my senior year. My professional goal was to become a process theologian. Vanderbilt, Claremont and Iliff accepted me to graduate school; and I was still pretty cocky. But the party ended in 1985.

Five years later, I awoke to find myself snatched away by the throes of mental illness. I awoke one morning vomiting severely in bed on a locked psych ward at St. John's Hospital in Anderson, Indiana. It would be nice to say that after I had put on my "Holy Spirit Decoder Ring" the Holy Spirit snatched me away from Denver to awaken pleasantly in Anderson. Also, it would have been nice if "Scotty" had beamed me up for a five-year vacation to explore the galaxy aboard the Mother Ship. But that's not what happened either.

No, when I woke up on the psych ward in 1990, I had just lived through the hells of five years of mostly untreated major mental illness, with symptoms of psychosis, mood and anxiety disorders. During those five years I lost everything I had once cherished. I lost my first wife. I lost my mind. I lost my friends. I lost the ability to read and write. I lost interest in performing even the most basic and menial tasks of self-care. I could not work and could not support myself. All I was capable of was being psychotic, and being ripped by complicating symptoms of mood and anxiety disorders. I had been snatched away from reality so far that I had lost my self. Somewhere along the way God was snatched away from me, too.

But with medication, individual counseling and group therapy, my mind started to return. The paranoid, grandiose, mood-distorted world I inhabited began to fade away. The delusional walls in which I lived started falling. Bit by bit I started to recover some sense of confidence and ambition.

Most powerfully, though, like many other consumers have found, I started to recover my essence, my spirit and soul, my heart and head, uniting in life-affirming hope and aspiration. How? In group therapy I rediscovered God; God rediscovered me; or, perhaps, we rediscovered each other--I don't know which and I don't know why. Regardless, in group therapy--a totally secular experience--God and I were reunited. Early on within the dynamics of group and peer interactions, I was convinced that God's healing spirit was at work...in me, in my peers, in the therapists and in my doctor. How odd, I thought, that these mental health professionals embodied the Creative Spirit of the universe. Despite the fact that most of them were not overtly religious or denominationally affiliated, the Breasted One--El Shaddai--enfolded me within Her healing bosom through their ministrations. It is likely that if I had not perceived God at work within them, I would not have complied with the court order that had committed me to their care. As is the case with many consumers, my spirituality was at the integral core of my recovery.

Nearly a year passed. In December of 1990 I was snatched away once more. I was in Denver, Colorado, getting ready to commence an MBA. But my hideous symptoms returned. My psychiatrist had just taken me off all my medications because he, my treatment team and I thought I had recovered 100%. But we soon learned we were very wrong. At dinner one night in Denver the delusions and anxiety returned, to snatch me away from my labors of recovery while dashing my hopes of getting an MBA. I was certain that the diners who had assembled that evening all had ESP (which I lacked) and were sending me coded messages through their casual banter and conversation with one another. Within myself I heard and felt my soul screaming with horrific terror. "God, why are they talking about me? Why are they saying I must give up my identity and assume the persona of another? Why can't I just be plain old Greg, who only wants to go to school, climb mountains and ski? Why are these people telling me I must assume an alien identity? Why? Why? Why? Why are these things happening to me again?" There were no answers, just silent screams.

Time had passed when I awoke. It was a hot summer night in 1991 and I could sleep no more. I was very hungry. I was a missing person, living in my car during one of my three homeless, extended "road trips." I woke up somewhere in Oklahoma at an interstate rest area. That night I suffered the first-known case of "Mad Cow Disease" in North America. For the past two weeks I had eaten just one meal a day because I was pretty much out of money--gas money, food money, precious money. I could no longer rely on using my maxed-out, delinquent credit cards. I was tired of eating the last of my rations--raw sweet potatoes. Everything else was gone.

I came to. I was in Oklahoma. I was in cattle country; and, "the cattle were lowing"--they were nearby. Then they struck: the first primal symptoms of Mad Cow Disease! My senses were peaking. All at once I surmised I could take the axe from my trunk and use it. My plan was to take my axe, drive to a rural cow pasture, and hunt for beefsteak! How exciting! My fast would soon end! I would take my axe and find the "fattened calf!" I would use the butt end of the axe to wallop a calf right on its noggin! Once unconscious, the calf would be mine. With the axe I could butcher a hindquarter. I would ice the beef in a trash bag, drive to a secluded place and enjoy some fresh meat!

I was alive! My hunger's end was near at hand! All I had to do was perform the task...rustle a calf, butcher a hind quarter, and roast some fine Oklahoma veal. "Rustle! Rustle? That's a crime! Damn! It won't work! I'll get caught! Crap! The bloody herd will start mooing and screaming when I hit the pasture; and that will wake up the rancher! Damn! I've got to be quick! But what about the calf's momma? She'll scream to high heaven when I get near her calf, let alone smack it! What's going to happen when I hit the stupid calf? Gees, the bloody calf will wail! The momma will scream! The herd will scream! I'll get caught! Hell, I'm in Oklahoma! They kill people for rustling!" Having been faced with certain death if I rustled some beef, I started to calm down. The symptoms of Mad Cow Disease went away; and I opted for a raw sweet potato...the fattened calf would grow up only to get fatter.

Another morning dawned, and I had been snatched again. That morning in the fall of 1991 brought no comfort on the psych ward, only more terror--searing, horrible, unrelenting terror; the kind of terror one can escape only when sleeping. My first stay on the psych ward one-year previously had been bad enough. Back then all I had to fear was being taken by a vampire. I couldn't commit suicide, even though I desperately wanted to. For I knew "they" (the vampires and their evil companions) would revive my brain and body, and punish me if I took my life. I knew that after they revived me they would do one of two things. Either they would preserve my brain in a jar and torture me for a thousand years; or, they would transmute my body into some form of oceangoing prey, which a predatory shark would play with and slowly devour.

This time it was worse. "They" were all around me. The other patients on the psych ward were merely disguised aliens; and in their human form they were cannibals. They were gathering for their mid-day meal. I panicked with terror whenever the lunch cart was late because they always got more vicious when they were hungry and unfed. I had to survive being their main course. How could I survive another such episode? At least once a day our meal cart was late. When it was late they paced voraciously. They stalked me right in front of the nurses' station. Like ravenous vultures, they circled and eyed their prey--me. The cannibal-aliens would fall upon me if our food did not come soon. But lunch came just in the knick of time; and once more I survived certain death.

There were other horrors and nightmares that racked me when I was awake. Aliens. They were everywhere. They were even _inside_ me--at least three different species contending for the mastery. These were all gestational, just like the kind that hunted "Ripley" (Sigourney Weaver in the movie series *Aliens*). I knew that one of them was the queen. She was biding her time; and taunting me while she kept me alive, at her will and whim. With her inside I knew there were two possibilities. I could either figure out how to get back aboard the Mother Ship; or, she would kill me. If I could just get to the elevator for "beam out" she would become my friend, ally and guide. If I could just get back to the bridge of my star ship. If I could only beam out and take my rightful place as Captain, her ESP would guide me as the greatest commander in the Galaxy! Like Noah of old, I would captain a great star ship--an ark, as it were. My ark would travel the Galaxy. My crew and I would discover and people new worlds--just like Noah and his family.

But I could not escape. The doors were locked. The windows were thick. I was three floors up; and the nurses had taken my only pair of shoes. I did not know the elevator's beam out code; and I was trapped! The second possibility seemed all but a foregone conclusion. I was convinced she would kill me and I would be her prey. I was horribly terrified. I surmised she would rip and tear through my chest; or I would be a meal for the cannibal-aliens. The aliens, who were all witches that could shape shift, would disguise themselves and leave...and I would have died, being remembered by none. Haunted by horror, these terrors lasted every day for many weeks; but I lived.

In June of 1999 I found myself. I was a Chaplain Intern at St. Elizabeths Hospital in Washington, DC. I had completed my MDiv. in 1996; and I had already completed three Units of CPE (Clinical Pastoral Education). My goal was to become a mental health chaplain. Little did I know that the time I spent at St. Elizabeths would turn out to be the most enjoyable year of my recovery.

Many treasures were found at St. Elizabeths. Each day I grew and became more whole. As a minister, as a chaplain, as a counselor, as a consumer, as a student and as a peer I was involved in a generative process of creative integration. For the first time, I was being treated with the latest and best of the newer atypical anti-psychotics and anti-depressants. With new medications, a very supportive environment, an invigorating educational setting, and marvelous opportunities for pragmatic ministries I began to start to trust myself and the world around me--as a soul who could dwell within a place of hope and hospitality. I was learning how to minister and provide spiritual care to the hospital's many consumers; who were themselves my greatest teachers. Now, at the age of 38, I was finally beginning to feel whole and connected to myself and to significant others around me. Life held forth promises for a hopeful, healthful future. Among many other accomplishments of which I am still proud, I became an ordained Minister of the Church of God.

However, the germ of integration at St. Elizabeths was a very small book I had brought with me from Indiana. A dear NAMI friend and advocate, Charles Kelly gave me a small book of essays entitled, *Religion and Disability*. Its three essays were written by Roman Catholic Donald Senior, Anglican John Macquarrie, and Protestant Stanley Hauerwaus- -all respected theologians. All three authors called for the full inclusion and acceptance of persons with disabilities into the life of the Church. Most exciting to me was their call for persons with disabilities to create theologies from the locale and circumstance of disability. This book is offered as an effort to develop the beginnings of such a theology from my perspective as a person who has been disabled by neurochemical disease.

St. Elizabeths was the perfect place to begin this constructive enterprise. I began to learn what it meant to *do* theology; to minister concretely to the many psychospiritual wounds of the hospital's many clients and consumers. Unique to this enterprise was the instructing chaplains' emphases upon finding viable mental health ministries based on the resources of Scripture and Christian tradition. Through class work, verbatim, sermons and opportunities to provide individual and group pastoral counseling, I was energized by the tasks of doing this sort of pragmatic theology. There at St. Elizabeths, I learned to use Judeo-Christian tradition to minister with the least of the least, those forgotten persons whose souls were tormented by the ravaging neuro-chemical imbalances of severe mental illnesses; those tortured souls who were so neglected, misunderstood, and delegitimated by most sectors of society.

At St. Elizabeths I found that I was a competent mental health chaplain. I found for the first time that my experience with disabling symptoms of severe mental illness was an asset. For although my clients knew not that I had mental illness, I knew them very well. I found that my sufferings could finally have meaning. I understood most intimately their terrors, their sadness, their anxiety, their worries, their marginalization, their poverty, and their loss of hope. I was becoming a "wounded healer" of the sort Henri J. Nouwen wrote about in his book, *The Wounded Healer.*

I also found that my previous academic and intellectual endeavors were excellent resources for ministry. I have been and remain fasci-nated by the field of hermeneutics, or the art of interpretation. I have been deeply influenced by Martin Heidegger, Hans Georg Gadamer, Michel Foucault, the New Hermeneutic, the Frankfurt School, feminist hermeneutics, and liberationist hermeneutics. I also consider myself to be something of an American Pragmatist cast in the philosophical the-ology based on the process philosophy of Alfred North Whitehead. So much for philosophical moorings. At the level of pastoral ministry and psychological investigation, I find myself to be most in debt to Anton Boisen, Wayne Oates, Heinz Kohut, Karl Jung, and Carl Rogers.

Without constructing an entire psychospiritual hermeneutic, I can outline some general features of the interpretative scheme I employ as a clinician and within this book. With Heidegger, I am fascinated by truth, *aletheia,* which is essentially disclosure or unconcealment. Texts, whether they be books or persons, are always to be interpreted; and that task is to bring to light what has been concealed, hidden or obscured. Gadamer's "fusion of horizons" is most profound. When people encounter one another or other texts, the act of understanding is one where horizons intersect. The interpreter of texts, or the counselor who interprets souls, lives within a horizon of meanings that define his/her identity. So too do texts and counselees. We all live within our particular horizons of meaning and identity. Understanding or the act of coming to truth (unconcealing the concealed) occurs when the individual horizons that separate people and other texts from one another fuse or meld. Understanding, or insight in psychological parlance, is thus a participatory activity in which all parties in conversation, dialogue, or counseling are mutually transformed. When horizons fuse, lives are transformed by the emergence of the truths that are revealed, manifested, realized and made known (Cf., Gadamer & C. Gerkin).

Foucault's archaeology of deconstructive power is seminal for its brute inevitability. In that vein Nietzsche's will to power is most intriguing as well. Power is a pragmatic reality that is highly constitutive of reality. "Chronically normal" people take for granted the ordering, systematizing, synthesizing, interpreting power of their neurochemically balanced brains. Not only are the majority of persons with severe mental illnesses economically and politically powerless, our neurochemically-disabled brains have lost their implicit power to shape, intend and understand the sensate world.

Foucault and Nietzsche can remind the interpreter that brains, texts and persons do not live on level playing fields where equal powers substantiate. Diagnoses, for example, can be power plays. Individuals and committees of clinicians determine diagnoses of symptoms, which define courses of treatment that have the power or force to incredibly alter the meaning of an afflicted life. I have a friend who was diagnosed with and treated for schizophrenia, yet never responded and remained highly symptomatic. His life's meaning and satisfaction were diminished by these *mis*diagnoses. However, when he received the correct diagnosis and treatment his life's satisfaction and meaning were immeasurably enhanced. Once diagnosed as having and being treated for bipolar illness, his psychoses and other symptoms were diminished and my friend's soul was restored. Make no mistake about it, diagnoses convey power. Accurate diagnoses and appropriate treatments have the power to renew and reinvigorate life's meaning for persons with severe mental illness. By the same token, misdiagnoses and the mistaken treatments they employ have the power to devalue, demean and diminish chances for health and recovery.

Foucault and Nietzsche also remind me of the historical inequalities of power that exist between those who diagnose and those who are diagnosed. In his masterpiece, *Madness and Civilization,* Foucault paints the stark picture of the European *Narrenschiff,* or Ship of Fools. Prior to the confinement of hospitals, Western Europeans casually and callously condemned persons with mental illness to these "ships of fools." Herded from the villages, hamlets and cities, persons with mental illness were confined to ships that bore them forever to the seas or to the major rivers. These insane "fools" were set upon ships to dwell alone until death took them at sea. Imagine living life's remainder upon a cold, damp, overcrowded, inhospitable ship, with insufficient food and nonexistent sanitation, racked by physical and neurochemical disease--never again to step on dry land, never again to feel the solid earth under one's feet and never again to see loved ones. Weakling "fools" were diagnosed by the powerful and treated like animals (Foucault, 1965, pp. vii, 7-13).

Foucault and Nietzsche's brutish fascination with power structures helps remind me how the history of the treatment of mental illness has largely been one of terror and torture. I give you the *Malleus Maleficarum,* or "Hammer of Witches." This book authored by pious Christians was used as a clinical manual to diagnose witchcraft. It was used for hundreds of years by Christian tribunals throughout Europe and the Americas to determine who was a witch. Suffice it to say that the cure for being a witch was usually torture followed by death--burning, hanging, quartering...whatever. The *Malleus Maleficarum* sent untold thousands to their death (Andreasen, 1985, p.145).

Students of the histories of psychology and of mental illness have revealed the horrific evil of this book's adjudicatory power. Oddly enough, this book reads like a primitive DSM IV--the clinical manual used currently by providers to determine diagnoses of mental illness. That is, the diagnoses of witches are parallel and identical to the categories we use today to diagnose specific mental illnesses. In short, the witches had mental illness. For example, "speaking to unseen demons or spirits" is equal to talking to "voices," which are the audible hallucinations that sometimes accompany psychosis. Thousands of miserable souls afflicted with untreated psychoses were condemned and burned as witches because their innocent conversations with "voices" were regarded as being hellishly demonic. Sometimes persons with bipolar illness can become over-stimulated sexually and promiscuous when untreated symptoms of mania prevail. In that regard, witches were said to be devilishly alluring figures of sexual attraction and engagement. Many men claimed they had committed adultery when they were cursed by a witch to have illegitimate sex. Thousands of manic souls were burned as witches because they could not control their symptomatic sexual drives and urges. Untold thousands of persons with untreated mental illness have been condemned as possessed witches to burn to death, at the hands of self-satisfying, powerful Christian tribunals. The Salem Witch Trials are a hideous example (*Ibid.*, p.145).

Foucault and Nietzsche remind us, too, that power structures render the control of discourse. The ability to speak and to define the terms of engagement can be a function of power. Long ago Socrates taught that the person of power was s/he who could define or name the terms of contraction, commerce and interaction. In *The Republic*, Plato himself stipulated that "justice is in the interest of the stronger." Power is a highly constitutive component within the construction of reality. We must be wary of the diagnostic powers we wield. For it is much too easy and all too common for clinicians and pastors to use language that shames and blames persons with severe mental illness--as though such sufferers have chosen their lot and are responsible for their conditions.

Whitehead serves to remind me that there are some gentler, more beautiful aspects of reality that are also constitutive of existence. The philosopher of process reminds us that the tender patience of divine love lures the world forward toward harmonious forms of life that embody and express enrichment, satisfaction, beauty, and creative advance. Change and process are constant. Becoming and advance are more constitutive than being and stasis. Such ennobling sentiment offers hope that recovery is possible for persons with severe mental illnesses. As our science and medical prowess advance, so increases the likelihood that new medicines and treatments will be found that can restore more of our ravaged brains and lives.

Regarding Boisen and Kohut, I spend more time outlining their contributions to my development and system later in the book. So allow me to say a few brief words about my indebtedness to Jung. Contra Freud, Jung believed that the religious impulse is not one of pathology; but is rather a component of human being that ennobles life toward wholeness, meaning and integration. The spiritual aspect of human being is one of seeking life's meaning and valuation within the forces of mystery and intuitive imagination. His concept of archetypes is foundational for my endeavors. My interpretations of the life of Boisen and the value of Kohut could not be suggested without my sense for the embodiment of the consistent systems of meaning that are archetypes. Also, there is my indebtedness to Jung that shows itself in my later portrayals of various Biblical characters.

I am also very much influenced by the thought and practice of Carl Rogers. For many years I have been convinced of the overwhelming significance of his reliance on and employment of empathy in the processes of client-centered therapy. "Rogerian listening" or empathic resonance is probably the most foundational clinical theory and practice I employ with my clients. There are several reasons for this. I think that I have found as most beneficial for me in my treatment have been those moments of empathic resonance, understanding, and acceptance I have felt as gifts offered to me by my clinicians, peers and chaplain supervisors. Being subsequently trained in supportive psychotherapy at St. Elizabeths, I gravitated towards that modality and continue to employ it due to its insistence upon the centrality of the healing power of empathic resonance and identification within the context of clinical-pastoral relationships. Such reliance on Rogerian structures and practices with some added pragmatics are central to my later definitions of clinical solidarity. It intrigues me that Rogers began his graduate career with studies in religion and divinity at Union Theological Seminary in New York City. I wonder how aware the mental health community is regarding the impact and significance of Roger's spirituality for the development and reliance on empathy that has become a central facet of clinical training and practice throughout the mental health community. It would seem that the ramifications of psychospiritual dynamics loom large, though sometimes obscured and forgotten.

The reader might wonder exactly what academics, ministry and psychiatric illness have in common. One might wonder what Heidegger, Whitehead, Boisen, and Kohut have to do with pastoral care, theology, and the experience of severe mental illness. My contention is that these seemingly disparate realities are actually of a piece. That is, in its essence, human being is the processive unity of psychospiritual quest and construction. The purpose of this book is thus to unconceal the essential unity of the psyche and the spirit, as portrayed in Judeo-Christian tradition; and as lived in the real experience of persons with severe mental illness.

The needs for this type of work are many. I begin with the problematic as felt by consumers. Many consumers in recovery cite their spirituality or faith as having been a chief force in, or even the major cause for their initial and sustained recovery. This fact is intriguing when one considers that religious preoccupations and delusions can be paramount experiences of consumers when we are symptomatic. It is furthermore intriguing when we realize that many religious persons, churches, faith groups, religious institutions, and pastors mistreat, reject and/or neglect our medical and psychological needs. It is furthermore disturbing to us that many secular mental health professionals eschew organized religion and matters of faith or spirituality. Some clinicians and their psychological traditions even view religious/spiritual experiences as symptomatic and pathological expressions of inauthenticity. The situation becomes more complicated when we recall that many conservative Christians regard psychological and psychiatric studies and practices as at best secular failures that neglect what they regard as the essential cause of mental illnesses, namely sin.

Nevertheless, we desire to receive psychological support for our spiritual needs and issues; and we desire to receive religious or spiritual support for our neurochemical dilemmas. Many of us want our treatment teams to accept and address us as spiritual persons; and we want our religious/spiritual friends to understand and help us with our neuropathology. But most often we get neither. Often enough behavioral and psychiatric communities turn their backs on our spirits; while spiritual persons and traditions turn their backs on our psyches.

There is thus a need for robust dialogue between practitioners of theology and students of psychology. I hope this book can contribute to the dialogues that are emerging between these disciplines. This book is intended as a spiritual and theological resource for health care professionals and students. It is simultaneously offered as a psychological resource for religious persons, communities of faith, and pastors. To both groups, I wish to herald the psychospiritual unity of human experience. It is my suspicion and contention that the psychological and spiritual poles of human existence cannot and should not be isolated or abstracted from one another. Each pole is a necessarily ingredient impulse of and for the other. They are inseparable poles within the ordering continuum that is human being. They constitute the essential framework within which the existential dilemmas of humankind are felt, defined, organized, confronted, and resolved.

Perhaps the greatest need this book meets resides in its self-serving character. I am interested and invested in this work as a consumer who needs and solicits mental health services. I am likewise a person of faith with spiritual needs. I write as a consumer addressing myself to fellow-consumers. I write in hope that my fellow sufferers can feel and become empowered by forcefully claiming the Bible and religious/spiritual traditions as being our very own. I will do this by demonstrating that the everyday experiences of persons with severe mental illnesses are not foreign to or forgotten by Scripture, tradition and the deity. In fact, our experiences are reflected within the mnemonic foundations of spiritual experience, tradition and Scripture. May the Spirit snatch us away from where we are; that we may later find ourselves to be relocated, recreated and reconstituted--all of us.

The man gave names to all cattle, and to the birds of the air, and to every animal of the field. Genesis 2:20

Chapter 2
What's In a Name?

From the outset, I declare a first principle. The essence of what it means to be human is that we are meaning makers. Meaning makers. We write stories. We tell tales. We write poetry, philosophy and theology. We write scientific journals. We write songs; and we sing songs. We write love letters; and we read love letters. We write legalese. We write mathematical treatises; and we write postulates of geometry.

We seek to understand…reality, one another and ourselves. We long for and create relationships that enhance life's pleasures. We celebrate birthdays, weddings, anniversaries, and other milestones. We grieve the experience of loss. *All* of these are activities that form meaning in our lives. One can even go so far as to say that the formation of meaning is essential to the construction of identity. We do these things, I believe, because we must. By virtue of being-human, we construe and construct the meaning-laden horizons of our existence. Perhaps this is some of what Heidegger intended by declaring that "language is the house of being." For regardless of whether one creates with a pen, via the tongue, or through heartfelt and relational experience, we humans dwell within the houses of texts, vocalizations, and relationships that convey our essence. To be human is to make sense of, to constructively identify, to shape reality, to encode meanings, and to define life's values. It is only in the forgetfulness of our essence as meaning makers that we fail to transcend yesterday's valuations with today's significance.

A favorite metaphor of meaning making resides in the poetic sentiment that humans are to "name the animals." Genesis 2:19-20 houses this sentiment within God's musings about what the human creature will do as essential human. Note therein, however, that God has not commanded the human to *do* anything. Rather, God waits to see what the human agent will do in its first moments of agency. Thus, as agent, defining its own identity-in-its-speech, the human being names all the animals that God has gathered for the human to see. As "namers of animals" we humans weave the fabrics of life's meanings, values and concerns as we shape, define, construe and intend to purport. As creative agents within the natural world, we interact with reality, ourselves, and God to construct what matters.

These reflections upon Genesis 2 are in debt to the work of process theologian Delwin Brown. He identifies Adam's task of "naming the animals" as an element within certain strands of Hebraic tradition that stress the importance and responsibility of human being's constitutive and contributive acts of naming. Brown suggests that, "Adam was to create an order, a system of meanings" (Brown, p. 9). By doing so,

Adam's creative construals reflect within him a sort of the generative energies that reside in God. Given God's musings about the goodness of creation, one suspects God felt glad to witness human being's emergent skills as a maker of meaningful enrichment.

For some time I have been grasped by Viktor Frankl's book, *Man's Search for Meaning*. Frankl's life and work have contributed much to my thinking about the human's capacity for creating meaning. For Auschwitz survivor Frankl, it is the striving and struggling for meaning that is the essential task and motivation of human being (Frankl, p. 121). He understood that one's valuations of life's meaning involve the entirety of human being's personality and identity. Thus, we see that meaning making is deeper than pure intelligence; more profound than emotional sentiment alone; more forceful than moral activity; and more creative than the fabrications of our hands. For all these dimensions--heart, soul, mind and strength--act in concert to produce the integrative value of life's meaning.

Perhaps this principle is operative within Jesus' equation of the two greatest commandments. In Matthew 22:37-39, Jesus states, "You shall love the Lord your God, with all your heart, and with all your soul, and with all your mind" (and with all your strength--my addition)..."and you shall love your neighbor as yourself." Herein we will find a holistic nexus within which we can define a trilogy of being and becoming where God, self and other are held in creative tension. While sometimes we might love ourselves more, sometimes love God more, or love our neighbors more, the human being always maintains creative tension with God and others. In one moment the meaning of God's love might predominate. In another moment one might find more meaning in self-nurture. At other times we might find that life's meaning is found more in our relationships with others. What we see is that love of God, love of self, and love of others involves our creative activity within a dynamic whose generativity involves at least these components: emotional formation of the "heart," spiritual formation of the "soul," intellectual formation of the "mind," and physical formation of "strength."

At various times in my life, one aspect of love (of God, of self, or of others) might have predominated above the others. At other times, I might have loved (God, self, or others) more emotionally; loved more spiritually; loved more intellectually; or loved more physically. But while focus and necessity might intensify one of these components, we humans always dwell within a complete horizon. This horizon empowers the creative tension that holds the dynamic of love of God, self and others, in context with our emotional, spiritual, intellectual and physical health. Thus, our construals of life's meaning are always acts of a whole person within his/her creative horizon. I am rather of the opinion that we function best as meaning makers when our hearts/emotions, souls/spirits, minds/intellects, and bodies/strength are at their optimum levels of integrative ordering. For optimum recovery and meaning making demand that one's emotions, one's thoughts, one's spirit, and one's body unite in healthy harmonies as stress and symptoms decline and are managed.

Perhaps it is the case that when we love life the most, we are at our most healthy. For it is very difficult to affirm life's value or meaning when we are alienated from our emotions; alienated from our spirits; alienated from our intelligence; and/or alienated from our bodies. Life's loss seems further intensified when any one (or more) of our relational dynamics are arrested. How can we love or value our own life's meaning if we cannot love God and others? What distorted meanings arise when God alone is loved to the exclusion of God's children--the self and the other? What perversities emerge if we are able to love only others, while denying care of ourselves and respecting God? Life's descent into darkness seems to further intensify when one's emotions, one's faith, one's reason, and/or one's actions fall victim to decay or mutagenesis. So it is with our experience of disabling severe mental illness. So it is for persons who suffer with catastrophic illnesses of other sorts. So it is for persons ravaged by life's inequities. I will thus develop further the notions that health can be equated with the experience of meaningfulness; and that illness can be equated with the experience of the pathetically absurd--meaninglessness.

A favorite, historic meaning-maker whom I admire as a self object is Anton Boisen. Born into a long-tenured, academic family, in the late 19th Century in Bloomington, Indiana, Boisen was a graduate of prestigious Union Theological Seminary in New York City. Boisen's profound autobiography, *Out of the Depths,* chronicles his life as a pastor, an academician, a foundational leader in pastoral care and education, and as a person who experienced severe mental illness himself--most likely bipolar illness. As such, Boisen is one of those few souls whose life-example is an ideal self object for me.

In October of 1920, Boisen had his first major "break with reality" and was accordingly hospitalized. As is the case with many of us, Boisen experienced some symptoms of severe mental illness that were extremely religious or spiritual in nature. During one of his first nights at Westboro State Hospital, Boisen experienced the joyful elation of hearing a choir of angels singing. He felt their "rhythm and beauty" everywhere; and, after they stopped, he felt them "hovering around the hospital"--as though they were safeguarding his arrival (Boisen, pp. 89-90). However, the following night was one of hellish terror and torment. Boisen states, "The next night I was visited...by a lot of witches" (*Ibid.*, p. 91). He heard constant, rhythmic, tap-tappings through a wall that he was certain were from evil agents seeking his location. His room began to stink from the smell of brimstone; and he was convinced that witches were gathering in the ventilator shaft to attack him. In his later reflections about these experiences, Boisen felt, "I had...broken an opening in the wall which separated medicine and religion" (*Ibid.*, p. 91). The significance of this constitutive act of interpretation resides in the specific empowerment it held for his life and career. For within his musings, Boisen recounts a delusional obsession he had concerning a vision of the cross and the moon. At one point he saw the "Moon... centered in a cross of light;" which was proof to him that his experiences were significant and paramount.

Therein we can see that Boisen's recovery was about to begin. As he reflected on the meaning of the moon and cross, he noticed he was looking at the moon through a hole in his window screen. Looking through the hole Boisen observed there was no cross--just a hole. This moment of clarity helped Boisen begin his journey of learning to distinguish delusions from reality. Glenn Asquith, editor of, *Vision from a Little Known Country: A Boisen Reader,* comments, "This realization contributed to his recovery; he suddenly came out of the acute disturbance much as one awakens from a bad dream. It was then he began to reflect on the meaning of his experience, that he found a new purpose in life and found a new understanding of mental illness" (Asquith, p. 6). In his own autobiographical account Boisen stated, "The cure has lain in the faithful carrying through of the delusion itself" (Boisen, p. 101). We can surmise that Boisen's insight was birthed via his unrelenting efforts to make meaning out of the absurd. For he was convinced there was an indissoluble element of valid religious experience resident in his symptoms of psychosis. Asquith comments thereabout that Boisen's efforts of "Finding out the meaning of these 'experiences,' led to a new purpose in life and to his eventual recovery and discharge from the hospital" (Asquith, p. 6). Certainly, Boisen's experiences of the angelic singing; the diabolical brimstone and witches; and his preoccupations upon the cross--all these were not simply symptoms. They became focal points of life-crises that needed to be healed via the infusion of value and meaning he would give them.

In, *Out of the Depths,* we see that the month of February 1921 was pivotal for Anton. In a letter to his mother, he recounts his awareness that he could not return to the parish after his experience of mental illness. Rather, he began vocalizing his desire that a career in mental health and religion was the path, "to take as my problem the one with which I am now concerned. That seems to me the clear course. It would give meaning and unity to the experiences of the past and provide something for me to live for and work for" (Boisen, p.110). Such resolve included Anton's burning desire to minister to the needs of persons with mental illness. He was convinced, "that many forms of insanity are religious rather than medical problems and that they cannot be successfully treated until they are so recognized" (*Ibid.,* p. 113). "Successful treatment" was based in part on Boisen's view, "...that there is no line of separation between valid religious experience and the abnormal mental states which the alienist calls 'insanity'" (*Ibid.,* p. 113)

The difference between pathology and valid religious experience meant for Boisen that pathologies recede, lose ground, and destroy personality. However, valid religious experiences convey and unify the force of healthy personality. Indeed, I owe to Boisen my views that health involves meaningfulness; while pathology is essentially absurd-- for so his experiences concord with my own. Thus citing the conversion/crisis experience of Saint Paul on the Damascus Road, Boisen could claim that Paul was a "religious genius," and not insane, because the Saint's (symptomatic) experiences resulted in a constructive outcome. This element of constructive integration via (apparent) psychopathology is connected to Anton's views regarding the ultimate meaning or purpose of one's life. Ever idealistic, Boisen claimed, "The end of life is to solve important problems and contribute in some way to human welfare, and if there is ever a chance that such an end could best be accomplished by going through Hell for a while, no man worthy of the name could hesitate for an instant" (*Ibid.,* p. 132)

Solving problems. Solving problems is what Boisen did. Solving problems is what persons with severe mental illness must do...if we are to recover with the catastrophes of our neuropathologies. Though we might sense a bit of grandiosity on his part, we can discern an important element of truth in Anton's declaration that he had broken the wall between religion and medicine. Prior to his leadership, religion and medicine were distanced even more than they are present-day. Boisen's leadership in bringing seminary students to hospitals for clinical education about the theological conundrum of health and illness was a first. Boisen is famous for coining the phrase that seminary students need to read and learn from "the living human document." By this he envisioned that the clinical education of students would rely on the honorable and pathos-laden self-declarations of afflicted human souls and bodies. How much better to learn about the real meaning of human struggle from a person who actually encounters such evil, than merely to read a (healthy) person's interpretations concerning the sufferings of a patient. Reading the "living human document" has thus become a principle ingredient in the clinical pastoral education of seminary students, ministers, and chaplains.

Asquith is quick to note that Boisen's clinical work as a chaplain was "focused on the religious meaning of individual suffering" (Asquith, p. 9). Asquith also claims that, "From Boisen's pastoral ministry-in-depth to the mentally ill, modern pastoral theology was born" (*Ibid.*, p. 9). Moreover, "Boisen's approach to empirical theology and the psychology of religion had a distinctively clinical, pastoral, and educational perspective which indeed made him the 'Father of the Clinical Pastoral Movement'" (*Ibid.*, p. 9). Indeed, Anton's life and work, as a person in recovery with (likely) bipolar disorder, was remarkable; especially when we consider that he lived during an era when psychiatric medications were not available. We would do well to honor his claim that he broke the wall between religion and medicine. For through his many labors, struggles and advocacy, he plowed the way through which much cross-fertilization between religious and medical studies has flourished.

One shall have noticed that I have referred to Anton as an "ideal self object." At this point I thus need to impart how and why I am using the phrase, "ideal self object." In his book, *Self Psychology and the Humanities,* Heinz Kohut reflects upon the meaning that courageous lives have for co-humanity. He asks, "What allows (or compels) some people to face death and even suffer it, rather than give up the openly professed loyalty to their ideals, to bear 'witness' in traditional religious terminology? In what consists the courage of those who, though outnumbered or alone, will yet maintain their self and their ideals" (Kohut, p. 5)? Kohut's analysis of courageous persons reveals that at critical, nodal life-points, such persons find strength beyond themselves, quite often through examples of other, previously courageous souls. For Boisen, a seed of courage germinated as he labored to understand what meaning a supposed cross-in-moonlight entailed for his life, work, and recovery. For Frankl, survivor of Auschwitz, the formation of life-sustaining courage was based on one's ability "to see a meaning in his life" (Frankl, p. 136). Such actions are witnessed in the choices of persons who can accept "this challenge to suffer bravely;" for by suffering bravely, "life has a meaning up to the last moment, and it retains this meaning literally to the end" (*Ibid.*, p. 137). In the concentration camps, Frankl knew many whose brave, honorable, and meaningful suffering could not be extinguished. In the halls of the psych wards, Boisen found meaning that enabled him to suffer bravely; and which gift he could share with others.

Obviously, the life forces of Boisen and Frankl resound within me via the force they have as self objects. According to Kohut, a principle means of healing the traumas of (legitimate) narcissistic injuries involves the wounded person's ability to allow another, a caregiver, to become his/her self object. Clinically, self objects are courageous caregivers whose capacities for empathizing with sufferers enable narcissistic injuries to heal (Kohut, p. 73). Via his clinical experience, Kohut came to learn that many of his narcissistically wounded clients formed a particular therapeutic alliance with him. He noted that some of his clients tended to invest themselves in his life as a psychological horizon in which to script the dramas of their inner souls. Kohut called this event one in which he became a self object for the wounded client. As an ideal self object in their therapy, Kohut observed that his clients' ability to find their own meaning and ideal existence within his acceptance enabled them to heal. This meant his ability to bear empathically the ideals of his clients helped empower their abilities to shore up personal coherence, find self-esteem, and function with greater harmony (Randall, pp. 35-39).

There are two reasons why Kohut's analyses of self objects are important to this book, this particular piece of meaning making. First, I am convinced that the onset of severe mental illnesses, our experiences of symptoms, and even recovery processes require our ability to heal via self objects. The empathy and compassion we might experience with a pastor, a friend, a counselor, or doctor are vital for the restoration of our souls and the healing of our wounds. We are strengthened to make meaning and to suffer bravely in the presence of supportive, empathic caregivers. This is so, I believe, because self objects can empower and inspire us to examine with courage the horrendous losses and damage to our (legitimate) narcissism. For we have many legitimate narcissistic wounds that result from the ravages of our symptoms and society's general stigmatizing of our conditions. Without such loving, sustaining, empathic others, our recovery would be less complete and certainly less meaningful. Hence, we note a powerful therapeutic "payoff" in our enhanced, meaningful recoveries when we experience such healthful, clinical self objects.

Secondly, I extend Kohut's clinical analyses of self objects to the realm of religious texts and persons. For I am convinced that religious figures can and do impart clinically verifiable benefits to sufferers, such as enhanced courage, optimal healing and increased meaning making. I am of the opinion that the psycholiterary examples of many Biblical characters are paradigmatic figures who function as (historic and ideal) self objects. Such historic-textual self objects can and do help us find courage to suffer bravely and to make significant, recovery-enhancing meaning out of the tragedies of our lives. In such persons, we see individuals who are like us, individuals who are able to inspire us to overcome our deficits because they have done so. Such convictions and analyses will help construe and fashion later portrayals of the importance of Abraham, Moses, St. Paul, and Jesus, who can become meaningful, ideal, historic, courageous self objects for us.

Then the Lord God said, "See, the man has become like one of us, knowing good and evil"...therefore the Lord God sent him forth from the garden of Eden...He drove out the man. Genesis 3:22-23

Chapter 3
Meaning Lost

Allow me to pose the question why (a) person(s) with severe mental illness should care about meaning making. Similarly, let us inquire what it might mean for clinicians to reflect on meaning making as a psychospiritual source of healing. The reason meaning making is so essential demonstrates itself precisely when we lose this ability. In my opinion, the onslaught and course of severe mental illnesses rob us of the ability to make meaning. Hence, when we become depressed, manic, anxious, obsessed, or psychotic, we lose what most people take for granted--we lose the exacting precision of being able to make sense out of life. This is because severe mental illnesses attack the primary functions of the organ we rely on most to interpret reality and construe life's meaning--the brain.

In her groundbreaking book, *The Broken Brain,* Dr. Nancy Andreasen, MD, sets forth a neurobiological and neurochemical account of the mental illnesses. While I intend to follow in brief her outline of neuropathology, I must admit that my cursory review of her neurochemical and neurobiological analyses is a gross oversimplification. But it can serve as a very basic introduction to the field of neuropathology. I also want to convey some of her views regarding symptoms of severe mental illness. This will be to amend and contend that the experience of symptoms of severe mental illness can disrupt and even destroy our ability to construe life's meaning as we attempt to interpret reality.

Let us begin by examining depression. The experience of depression is ultimately one of mood or affect. Yet, the healthy regulation of mood and affect depends on the neurochemical balance of two major, interactive neurotransmitters: norepinephrine and serotonin. Early research on the action of the older tricyclic and MAO anti-depressant medications indicated that these classes of drugs increased the amount of norepinephrine in the central nervous system. It was soon realized that increased levels of norepinephrine available to the brain decreased the experience of symptoms of depression. Early research also demonstrated the importance of the neurotransmitter serotonin in regulating depression. For it was observed that early anti-depressant medications stimulated the release of serotonin (*Ibid.*, pp. 231-234). I might add that since this book was published a new class of anti-depressants was engineered. Such meds as Zoloft and Prozac are called SSRI's--selective serotonin reuptake inhibiitors. Their unique action is to prevent neurons from taking back levels of serotonin that have been released. By blocking the reuptake of serotonin, the amount of serotonin available in the brain is increased, which decreases the symptoms of depression.

When such neurotransmitters as norepinephrine and serotonin are out of balance, persons with depression feel "sad, despondent, 'down in the dumps,' blue and full of despair and hopelessness" (Andreasen, p. 41). Anxiety, acute psychoses, and/or somatic problems can also accompany depression. For example, when persons are depressed, Andreasen notes marked disturbances in sleep patterns. One person might not be able to fall asleep. Another person might wake up frequently in the middle of the night. Others might wake up early and be unable to return to sleep. Still others might need to sleep almost constantly--rarely venturing forth from bed (*Ibid.*, p. 42).

The essential distortions of depression are equally troublesome. Depression can include the loss of interest in activities one previously found to be enjoyable or meaningful. Participation in sports, social functions, school, dating, traveling, reading, etc., can stop entirely when one is depressed. It is not uncommon for previously gregarious folk to avoid established, trusted friends and/or avoid making new friends or acquaintances.

Another characteristic of depression is the symptom of anhedonia--the loss of the ability to feel joy or pleasure. This is when a person cannot find comfort or pleasure in events that normally bring joy. For example, the depressed person might feel no joy in the birth of a child; or no joy in getting a raise. Watching sports could be totally boring or even distressing. Loss of physical, mental and/or emotional energy can

35

also occur during depression, such that a person always feels lethargic, unmotivated or "drained." Even the ability to concentrate can be impaired when one is depressed. For example, some people with depression complain of being unable to follow or track the action-events of a sports contest. One might even be unable to follow a favorite storyline in literature or other media. Losses of self-confidence in one's abilities to work, shop, access community resources, or even clean house can also occur (*Ibid.*, pp. 42-43).

In view of these clusters of symptoms, I contend that when one is depressed these symptoms impede and negate one's otherwise tacit abilities to make meaning. For example, the loss of interests or pleasurable activities interferes with the delight and satisfaction that normally accompany joy-in-doing. Doing things that make us feel good is a primary source of healthy meaning making. When depressed, though, we lose the meaningful experiences of contenting events and activities. Imagine a person who, when not depressed, is gregarious; but when depressed isolates him/herself from friends, family and meaningful relationships. Such depressive isolation robs such persons of being able to engage in the formation and sustenance of relationships that help make life worthwhile.

The experience of depression's avolition, lethargy, and lack of motivation include an insidious assault upon one's levels of mental, emotional and physical energy. From the perspective of an untrained, inexperienced observer, it often appears that depressed people are just plain lazy. But the truth of the matter is more disarming. For persons with depression have not chosen to be lazy, lethargic, avolitional or un-motivated. Rather, when depressed, the neurochemical character of the illness itself robs one of energy. Consider that when depressed a person cannot get enough sleep or cannot sleep much at all. In themselves, both extremes deplete one of his/her essential energy. Also, in general, depression destroys one's energy-abilities that otherwise provide and create meaningful experience.

For example, try to imagine being a student. It takes a certain amount of sustainable energy to read, to study, to write papers, and to prepare for and take tests. Most students who succeed have enough en-ergy to perform such tasks; and they are generally motivated to achieve and perform. Such achievements and performance levels include one's delight with success, which make for meaningful educational oppor-tunities. However, imagine being so depressed that one doesn't have the energy to get out of bed to go to class, to read, to study, or to write. Imagine being so lethargic that one quits reading one's favorite texts and subjects--only because these previously meaning-producing events are now monumental tasks that intimidate, overwhelm, and/or frighten the depressed person. What was once fun and energy invoking has now become a tedious labor that creates an energy drain from just thinking about doing it, let alone actually attempting to perform. The loss of motivational energy thus impedes, impairs and denies the abilities of persons with depression to perform many functions that otherwise pro-duce meaningfulness. Thus, the meanings of depression are distorted deprivations: despair, sadness, hopelessness, lethargy, anhedonia, lack of motivation, avolition, isolation and impaired concentration--hardly the stuff of meaningful experience.

Bipolar illness can be an experience of frantic uncertainty. For the afflicted person has to deal with mood swings between mania (elation) and depression (sadness).

These mood swings and other major symptoms of bipolar illness involve the interplay of three major neurotransmitters. Serotonin levels impact depression, stability of mood and aggression/impulsivity. While dopamine has been identified as significant in terms of the processes of schizophrenia and psychosis, it is also related to the experience of mania.

As we have seen earlier, norepinephrine levels can impact depression. Recent research also demonstrates that the symptoms of bipolar illness actually decrease and destroy nerve cells in various areas of the brain. Thus, studies of the action of lithium on bipolar illness suggest that lithium has neuroprotective properties as well as abilities to induce the growth of new neurons. In addition to neurochemical and cellular defects in the brain, many studies have demonstrated that there are genetic predispositions for the onset of bipolar illness (Fawcett, et al, pp. 52-54, 63-65).

If one's manic experiences were purely, merely expansive, pleasant moods, few would ever complain. Boundless energy, goodwill, heightened ambition, and enthusiasm would be a great way to feel (*Anderson*, p.45). For during such manic phases, much of society's excellent, creative genius has been produced. Van Gogh's artwork reflects both his depressive and manic experiences. The force of the Protestant Reformation would have been diminished were it not for the violent, sometimes caustic mood swings of Martin Luther's bipolar illness (*Ibid.*, p. 51). We can say that this creative aspect of bipolar illness is sometimes a friend to meaning making. For example, Johns Hopkins Professor Kay Redfield Jamison--herself a sufferer of bipolar illness--recounts how when untreated and manic she could write scads of papers within drastically short periods of time (Jamison, pp. 131-132). Moreover, she is recognized as being America's leading expert on the treatment and diagnosis of bipolar illness. She has found continued success, though, only by recognizing her ongoing and continual need for medical treatment. There is indeed an enhanced capacity for some persons with bipolar illness to be particularly creative and even genius.

But manic phases never remain euphorically benign; and because they don't, genuine meaning is distorted. Usually, the experience of mania will include a happy, grandiose elevation of mood that can include irritability, poor judgment, and extreme impulsiveness. Sometimes persons with bipolar illness will even experience the horrors of psychotic symptoms. Thus, we see that the pathological character of mania negates the healthy formation of meaningful experience. Consider that when euphoric and grandiose a person with mania exercises impulsive, poor judgment. Such periods notoriously undermine the normal flow of life events. For manic, impulsive, poor judgment can manifest in the ill person spending $25,000 on a new automobile that s/he cannot afford. Some manic persons have been known to rack up thousands of dollars in debt by impulsively leaving families and work to go on lavish vacations, which they can ill afford. Also, some persons with mania have been known to charge thousands of dollars on their credit cards in just a few wild days of shopping--for things s/he would otherwise not likely need, let alone purchase (Andreasen, p. 48).

Add to these considerations that impulsive, poor judgment can include the reckless and dangerous expressions of unrestrained sexual encounters. Feeling euphoric, elated and aroused, some persons with mania will seek out and endulge sexual appetition at levels they would consider excessive when otherwise healthy. Also, manic phases can impede one's business judgment. For instance, when manic a person might risk thousands of dollars or entire life savings on shady or shaky business ventures--for example, speculating on stock, or getting into real estate, etc. Unfortunately, such examples of the pathology of mania can last for periods of days or even weeks, compounded by little or no rest (*Ibid.*, p. 48).

Though we have spent previous time examining unipolar depression, a few comments are in order regarding depression within the context of bipolar illness. The pathologies that define depression still operate in bipolar illness. However, there are some anomalies. For some unfortunate souls are "rapid cyclers"--which means they move in and out frequently between manic and depressive phases quite often without clue, rhyme or reason, just random cycling. Also, when depressed the previous euphoric poor judgment has relented; such that the now depressed person might regret and mourn the consequences of his/her poor, impulsive judgments (*Ibid.*, p. 51).

What should be made clear about bipolar illness is that its particular absurdities distort meaning making in some unique ways. If a person with mania is experiencing symptoms of thought disorder or psychosis, then s/he has likely entered a completely surreal landscape wherein normal rules of perception and cognition are non-applicable. That is, one's abilities to perceive and order the immediate realities of life's intensities are themselves diminished.

There seem to be some other, rather insidious and destructive forces in bipolar illness that assault and decrease one's ability to make meaning. Uncertainty is a terrible thing; and for some souls, who suffer with manic depression, uncertainty rips one's meaning-laden world apart. We tend to trust that which is stable, sure, reliable, comforting and normative: order. We tend to distrust that which is disordered, disharmonious and chaotic. Regrettably, many persons with bipolar illness live with the meaning damaging consequences that result from the uncertainty and untimeliness of one's mood swings. This uncertainty factor can shatter meaning making because one cannot trust the reality in which one dwells. One fears whether s/he will be in a manic mood today. S/he fears that s/he might be overwhelmingly sad today. Perhaps s/he will contend with irritable mixed mania-depression. Cycling through the uncertainties of moods and symptoms of bipolar illness negates our trust-formations and meaningful interpretations of our life-worlds and interactions.

Perhaps the form of mental illness that is most destructive of one's meaning making capacities is schizophrenia. The first neurotransmitter to be implicated in schizophrenic processes was dopamine. The "dopamine hypothesis" suggested that schizophrenia involved the hyper-transmission and over-supply of dopamine in the brain's system of neuropathways. The first verifications of this theory came from an analysis of the older (typical) anti-psychotic medications. It was discovered that these medications blocked a specific dopamine receptor (the D2 receptor) that moderated and reduced the disabling symptoms of schizophrenia. Hence, scientists have learned that a major player in schizophrenia is the excessive transmission of oversupplied levels of dopamine to an abnormally overabundant number of dopamine receptors (*Ibid.*, pp. 222-225). In recent years, though, scientists have also discovered that the neurotransmitter serotonin is involved in the illness of schizophrenia. Hence, the newer atypical anti-psychotic medications target both dopamine and serotonin systems that has revolutionized the treatment of schizophrenia. The brains of persons with schizophrenia have also been shown to possess structural abnormalities, via such methods as postmortem research and neuroimaging. Additionally, there appear to be genetic and hereditary factors that are involved in schizophrenia (*Ibid.*, p.225-230).

Symptoms of schizophrenia can include: paranoid delusions; grandiose delusions; religious delusions; audio/command hallucinations; tactile hallucinations; chronic depression; avolition; isolation; and others. When untreated or mistreated, one's delusions during acute psychosis are very real and rigidly held by the ill person. Although to one's friends, family or clinical team an ill person's claim, "I am Jesus" is patently false, to the delusional person the declaration, "I am Jesus" conveys the full force of truth that his/her mind will permit. Thus, it sometimes takes families and clinicians long periods of time to stop trying to "reason" or "speak logically" to such ill persons. The harder a "sane" person argues or "reasons" with a person in psychosis, the more agitated the person can become and the more entrenched s/he will be in holding on even more rigidly to his/her distorted thoughts. For untreated delusions and psychoses are rigidly held, fixed and totally real to the afflicted person (*Ibid.*, p. 60).

Our abilities to perceive and conceive reality's meaning obviously shape and inform our identity. Psychotic distortions and symptoms negate otherwise healthy interpretations and significations to the extent that they can destroy ill persons' identities. Consider the meaning of a life of an "insane"/absurd self. I mentioned earlier that at one point I was totally convinced that an "alien queen" was lodged in my chest. It took several months with meds, inpatient, and outpatient treatment for me to become stable enough to be free of such terrifying thoughts. During that period of time I suffered unrelentingly from this paranoid system of delusions, among others. The only peace I felt was when I could sleep. Otherwise, I was terrified of being killed by the alien every waking moment of every torturous day. During this time my sense of identity as a healthy, functioning person was lost. I was incapable of accessing previously meaningful roles and identity. I was incapable of being a student. I was incapable of being an athlete. I was incapable of being an employee. I was incapable of being a spouse. I was no longer a son or brother within a family. Such roles of defined, meaningful existence were completely lost. I was totally and completely a person who was about to be killed by aliens--nothing more, nothing less. In brief, untreated psychoses can completely destroy the normal, healthy self one was, while replacing a healthy identity with pseudo, fictitious self-understandings. Psychoses can destroy the identity bases of the afflicted, as they destroy the healthy self's ability to construct meaningful horizons of existence in which the identity may dwell and define itself.

Some other meaning distorting characteristics of psychoses can be further noted. Sometimes we believe thoughts are being planted in our minds. This can involve one's (mistaken) belief that s/he is receiving and/or sending ESP messages of which others are distinctly aware. Such secrets can be transmitted by any media, including radio, TV, print or via the mind itself; and such symptoms are clinically defined as being ideas of reference. Quite frequently ideas of reference can include the experience of one believing, even perceiving that his/her mind is being "read" by others, as though one's thoughts were being stolen and unjustly disclosed to others.

Within these characteristics of delusions I see distortions of reality that render an ill person's experience of life as absurd. The absurd is meaningless. The experience of symptoms of severe mental illness is absurd. There is no healthy meaning within a self that has felt itself become an absurdity. Persons with severe mental illness can become so empty that we lose even the sense that we are victims. By our illnesses particularly, and society's treatment of us in general, we are violated, victimized, disrespected, negated, abused and tormented. Such are the distortions that define the absurd, the unreal, the unreasonable, the meaningless.

There are yet other symptoms of schizophrenia that destroy the self and its meaning making capacities. Hallucinations are another set of perceptual/conceptual anomalies (*Ibid.*, pp. 60-61). One friend of mine often reported seeing a ravenous tiger stalking him down the street. But just when he thought an attack was near at hand the tiger started talking to him, sharing secret and fantastic information. Hallucinations can obviously be incredible, terrible, terrifying distortions and disruptions to the normal sensate world of experience. In the book and the movie, *A Beautiful Mind,* John Nash experienced full-blown hallucinations in which he was (with grandiosity) recruited by clandestine government operatives to decipher and break Cold War Era Soviet codes. Yet, he also experienced the commingling of delusional and hallucinatory symptoms. For example, he believed he was being watched, antagonized and spied upon by both US and Soviet agents.

I have to imagine that the experience of dwelling within horizons distorted by full-blown delusional systems and hallucinations in tandem would be world shattering. Together I must believe they must be an experience of evil most heinous. For in such situations one's total sensory-perceptual grid would be entirely short-circuited. Instead of walking through a peaceful wood on a lovely fall day, imagine trudging through a forest in which demonic-appearing, winged bat-creatures attack and persecute one with shrieks of certain death. Unfortunately, such are the realities of an untreated, neurochemically unbalanced brain and mind.

Untreated schizophrenia is an evil that roughly one percent of the world's population experiences. It is in my purview an experience in which the meanings of "normal" sensate data are completely lost within a totally distorted horizon of experience. Many people with schizophrenia have shared how untreated psychoses are the most hellish of experiences, terrifying, torturous distortions in which healthy meaning is destroyed by neuropathology.

I have met and ministered with homeless persons who have suffered terribly from untreated schizophrenia. One of my friends moved to America from Ethiopia and left his family and his career as an educator due to the paranoia of schizophrenia. His delusions and hallucinations convinced him that he could escape the terrors of his small village by coming to America. However, his persecutions were even more intense and sinister when he arrived in Washington, DC. For there he began to believe that secret agents from his homeland were colluding with American agents to prevent him from finding a new life, work, and meaning. His psychoses rendered him a homeless street person who barely survived by eating once or twice a day at "soup kitchens," with no shelter from the elements. For him the normal sorts of meaningful banalities were rendered unavailable--he was alone, without friends or family, unable to work, confused and tortured by persecutory delusions and terrifying hallucinations that only reinforced the system of meaningless, absurd existence which was his. Obviously, symptoms of schizophrenia render life, identity, perception, relational satisfaction and simple pleasure as being impossibilities replaced only by the meaningless horrors of absurdity.

The last syndrome of severe mental illness I will discuss concerns the very broad spectrum of anxiety. The brain's GABA system plays a major role throughout the spectrum of anxiety disorders. In general, the GABA system of neurotransmitters has an overall inhibitory effect within the brain. It is thought that the GABA system works to exert a modulating or slowing down of other neurochemical systems. Hence, anti-anxiety drugs work to enhance the GABA system's moderation of other over-stimulated neurochemical systems. The discovery of the so-called "benzodiazepine receptor" indicated to researchers that there are specific receptors to which the anti-anxiety agents bind. This development suggests that the brain has its own system of inhibiting receptors that regulate its own neurochemical control of the over arousal involved in states of anxiety. In addition to neurochemical pathology, anxiety involves genetic predispositions and environmental/physical factors (*Ibid.*, pp. 239-241).

Freud helped us better understand the subjective experience of persons who experience anxiety. He rightly identified that when anxious, one can feel debilitating fear, personal terror, panic and doom (*Ibid.*, p. 63). Other psychological symptoms of anxiety can include: tension, nervousness, hyper vigilance, and being easily startled. In themselves alone, these clusters of problems could be experienced as certainly overwhelming and unmanageable. However, in addition to the subjective, psychological symptoms of anxiety there are complicating physiological symptoms that accompany this type of mental illness. The physiological domain of symptoms can include: racing heart, rapid pulse, chest pains, restricted breathing, suffocation, sweating, tingling, and tremors of the extremities, weakness, and others (*Ibid.*, pp. 63-64).

Though there are several distinct diagnostic categories of anxiety, I will focus only on one of them--obsessive-compulsiveness. Obsessive Compulsive Disorder (OCD) can be a truly debilitating, handicapping illness. In severe cases its victims can become totally disabled. This is due to the insidious severity of the interactions between the two poles of this illness-- obsession and compulsion. The obsessive feature of this diagnosis is a cognitive-mental dynamic wherein one has (a) thought(s), or systems of thoughts upon which one's ruminations can be almost constant. The compulsive dynamic is a performative-behavioral activity wherein one must act or do something. Together, obsessiveness and compulsiveness interact in ways that can be most crippling, as they can and do negate normative activities of healthy meaning making.

As an example, let us imagine the duress experienced by a person ravaged by this condition. Some severe cases of OCD involve compulsive behaviors that are insidiously ritualistic. It might take a person two hours to wash his/her hands just to prepare to eat breakfast, every day and every morning. Within such rituals are imbedded the tedious and monotonous repetitions of seemingly insignificant activity. The hands must be washed ten times with cold water, then dried with a clean towel that has been freshly laundered. Unfortunately, the hands soil the towel so that now the hands must be washed ten more times, but this time with warm water. After turning off the warm water, the now soiled towel must be laundered immediately. In such a performative ritual there might also be extreme time limits within which the hand washing, laundering, and turning off of water must be accomplished. If our hand-washer were too fast, or too slow, there would arise another set of compulsive behaviors to perform. Given that such rituals might last several hours, it is easy to see how seemingly banal activities become preponderant monsters. For example, eating breakfast becomes an additional two-hour ordeal involving rituals to prepare one's food, to clean one's hands, to clean one's utensils, and finally to clean the kitchen. Brushing one's teeth after breakfast could itself take one hour; and could be subject to another two-hour hand washing scenario. Obviously, the amount of time that such rituals take to perform would render it nearly impossible for a person to hold full-time, gainful and meaningful employment; as work time is lost to the time that is slavishly, unrelentingly devoted to the compulsive behaviors and activities.

But there is also involved the other polar dimension of OCD--its obsessive component. Obsession refers to a particular rigidity of thought upon which one cannot but ruminate and dwell. For example, an obsessive system of thought that could accompany the hand washing compulsion might revolve around a constant fear of getting cancer. In his/her mind, our sufferer might be convinced s/he must wash her/his hands in specific ways to ward off the possibility of getting lethal cancer because the only safeguard against getting the disease is to remove with exacting precision the cancerous laden filth that accumulates on his/her hands. Perhaps the fear of carcinogens in her/his food drastically limits what foods can be eaten and how they may be eaten. Also, s/he might surmise that cancer could only be further avoided by cleaning one's hands, utensils and table with exacting precision, while preparing to brush one's teeth to avoid oral cancers.

What we see in OCD, then, are the terrible interactions between compulsive behaviors and obsessive thoughts. These pathological polarities reinforce themselves and one another via feedback mechanisms. An example could be that a brave effort by our two-hour hand-washer to try to wash only once would create an avalanche of anxiety. For if the compulsion to wash is disobeyed, his/her obsessive thoughts can spike an intensely pitched anxiety during which one would necessarily die from cancer within one minute of failing to wash. Only as long as the compulsive rituals are obeyed and performed can the intense anxieties of obsessiveness be minimized and lessened. Likewise, any effort to deconstruct the cognitions of obsessiveness can result in a spiked interest to immediately perform the rituals of compulsion.

The impact of OCD on meaning making can be hauntingly severe. We have to ask what sort of meaningful life can be lived or considered possible by a person who is trapped inextricably by the insidious interactions of obsession and compulsion as defined above. Trapped at home; unable to work; stripped of social commerce; lacking family support or understanding; and living with a constricted diet, our friend with OCD is disabled by symptoms that negate the ebb and flow of meaningful, normative life-activities and interests.

Come no closer! Remove the sandals from your feet, for the place on which you are standing is holy ground. Exodus 3:5

Chapter 4
On Holy Ground
(Crises, Conversions and Self-Objects)

To begin this chapter, I wish to make an appeal on behalf of consumers who suffer with severe mental illnesses. Please treat our psychospiritual experiences as though you were treading on holy ground. I ask you to treat our vulnerabilities, insights and needs with hallowed respect. When you walk with us, let us walk together as though upon holy ground; even as God met Moses on holy ground. For we offer rare gifts and pearls of self-disclosure when we honor you with our stories and symptoms.

Let us start our walk as we "stand on holy ground" with Moses when the great prophet first meets God. In Exodus 3:1-6, we have a foundational stratum of God's covenant with Israel. As such, we also witness in Exodus a scriptural fascination with psychospiritual realities and anomalies. The founding event here is Moses' first encounter with God--in the wilderness. In Exodus 3:2, we read that an angel from God appears to Moses in a burning bush. We note that Moses is fascinated, tantalized and intrigued by this psychoreligious event. He is amazed to see a bush that burns, but which is not consumed by its flames.

The experience of having visual hallucinations can be quite distressing to persons who suffer with severe mental illness. One of my friends would occasionally see a tiger walking down Main St., which terrified him. Another friend saw the stars form an apparition of a wolf's head. Responses to such hallucinations are varied. They can include fear, paranoia, interest, inquisitiveness, euphoria, or even humor. Nevertheless, the distresses wrought by a burning bush or by configurations of stellar images occur because such events are not at all normal.

I know for a fact that if one of my clients claimed to see a burning bush that didn't die out, I would likely report a symptom of thought disorder or psychosis to our team and psychiatrist. S/He in turn would likely take steps to treat such an experience with a medication adjustment and other treatment modalities. But our society shames persons who have visual hallucinations because our experience of such events is regarded as "whacko" and includes the stigmatic judgment that we are unnatural and weird.

Even so, the Bible is a favorite book for many consumers; and we implicitly hold to it as authoritative for and formative of our faith. I think I have some insight as to why this is so. There is a very fine line between the portrayal of authentic religious experience and the experience of many symptoms of severe and persistent mental illness. In "our world," reading a story about the great prophet Moses seeing and talking to a burning bush is commonplace. For many of us see things and talk to various "voices" each and every day. Some of us can even spot plants that possess telepathic sentience with which our minds can meld. So for us, reading about Moses and his burning bush is very much a story about us. It is a sacred tale to us and about us because we correctly intuit that our psychoses and symptoms are not lost to God and the Bible. Rather, given the fine line between religious experience and symptoms of mental illness, we sense and intuit that God and the Bible love us precisely because our symptoms are similar to and not forgotten by the scriptural recollections of psychospiritual phenomena. The Bible fascinates us because we tend to see our pathologies mirrored in such foundational, theologically constructive events as Moses and the burning bush.

In verses 4-6 of Exodus 3, a second psychospiritual drama unfolds. In this vignette, Moses hears the "voice" of God. We, too, many of us, have heard the voice of God. But we are told that such "voices" are symptoms of our psychoses. One of my clients lamented as follows. "Chaplain, Abraham talked with God; Moses talked with God; and Mohamed talked with God. Why is it when God talks to me they make me take haldol?" (Note: haldol is an extremely powerful antipsychotic medicine with some nasty side effects.) Another friend of mine observed, "When we talk to God it's called prayer. But when God talks to us it's called schizophrenia." Not completely dissimilar from the traumas we experience with our "voices" (i.e., audible hallucinations); Moses became somewhat paranoid as he looked upon a burning bush through which the voice of God spoke to him.

At the moment we look back at God's discourse in verse 5 of this chapter. Moses is instructed by God to remove his sandals, "for the place on which you are standing is holy ground." I contend that this "voice" from God foreshadows Moses's return to the Sinai wilderness where the Ten Commandments will be received. God's "voice" also functions at a psychospiritual level to inform us that our experiences with symptoms of psychospiritual pathology occur in sacred time and space upon holy ground.

Exodus 19 intensifies the drama of covenant being built between the Hebrew people and God. The central characters in this chapter are Moses and God. Again, Moses hears the "voice" of God; this time commanding Moses to inform the Hebrew people that they are to obey God. Particularly, they are told to "obey the voice of God," primarily as heard by Moses. It is fascinating that religious leaders have been historically legitimated as authoritative persons of faith precisely because they are so attuned to God's voice. Perhaps the difference between a shaman, or holy person, and a person with psychosis is more a matter of degree than kind. That is, there is a fine line between religious experience and symptoms of severe mental illness.

Exodus 20:18-19 is fascinating in terms of the terror the (common) Hebrew people experience from God's noisy commotion when delivering the Ten Commandments to Moses. The "rank and file" are so terrified in this divine (psychospiritual) drama that they demand Moses to be their mediator with God and God's voice. They cry, "You speak to us, and we will listen; but do not let God speak to us or we will die." Serious matters are these encounters with the "voice" of God--powerful enough to threaten, overwhelm and terrify, powerful enough to result in death. Imagine the courage we are required to muster to help us cope with the terror and despair wrought by our hallucinations and "voices." It takes incredible courage and fortitude to survive our daily traumas, terrors, fears, insecurities and despair. Perhaps we can find Biblical hope in the person of Moses, who hears voices similar to ours, who see visions similar to our visual hallucinations. Perhaps there is hope in regarding Moses as a heroic self object for us. Perhaps there is hope for consumers in this portrayal of Moses. Might we dare to hope that our struggles, like those of Moses, could contribute to our well being and to the good of society? For in Moses, we can see am image of someone whose religious experiences are similar to our psychospiritual symptoms. Moses survived them and became a better leader because of them. I hope that our faith communities and treatment teams will regard our recovery with such devastating symptoms as worthy of moral respect, as they walk with us on holy ground.

Unfortunately, when the words "mental illness" are uttered, most chronically normal people translate that phrase into the debasing, stigmatizing word "psycho." Alfred Hitchcock's movie, "Psycho" went a long way to convey that mental illness is synonymous with "murderer," "deranged killer," or "maniacal serial killer." For reasons I don't quite understand, these most unholy epithets stigmatically characterize us as being the most lethal and dangerous members of society. Such stigma also functions to keep society from walking with us on holy ground. For when some poor soul who happens to have a mental illness does kill someone, the media blitz has a feeding frenzy in which the perpetrator's mental illness is played like a trumpet. Of course, such frenzies serve to caricature further the sentiment that persons with mental illness are the most violent and dangerous members of our society.

I must admit, though, there is a grain of truth in this assessment of our afflictions. It is true that, sometimes, persons with severe mental illness do kill other people--often people we love. But this understanding is only a half-truth. Almost 100% of the time, when persons with severe mental illness commit murder, they are doing so as the result of not being actively and aggressively treated for their disorder. When we have killed it is because we have not been treated appropriately with medication. A truth that few outside the mental health community are aware of is that when persons with severe mental illness are aggressively treated with proper psychotropic medication we are less likely than the average citizen to kill or commit a violent crime. In fact, clinical statistics indicate that when we are properly medicated, persons with severe mental illness are much more likely than the average citizen to be victimized by violent crime. Let me repeat this fact. When we are on meds, we are less likely than the average Jo(e) to kill or commit violent crime. When we are on meds, we are much more likely to be the victims of violent crimes than the average Jo(e).

One devastating symptom of untreated psychosis is called a command hallucination. When a person with untreated or mistreated psychosis hears a command hallucination, s/he hears a "voice" telling him/her to do something or to perform some act. These commands occur throughout a broad spectrum. One might be commanded to take a bath. One might be commanded to walk the dog. One might be commanded to shout. One might be commanded to commit suicide. One might be commanded to take the life of another person. These symptoms are obviously powerful and can be insidious. They generally occur when we are not properly medicated; and they occur with such forceful impulse that one dare not disobey them. For quite often, these heinous "voices" have a self-reinforcing feedback loop. That is, persons who hear such commands have been "trained" by their "voices" to obey without question. If one tries to resist the "voice" and its command, another "voice" can be heard which threatens to punish the afflicted. Disobey, and the "voices" get worse and more sinister. Obey the command, and the "voices" relent.

Given this brief analysis of command hallucinations, I will fashion a reading of Genesis' portrayal of Abraham's near sacrifice of his son, Isaac, as being another one of those examples in which only a fine line separates religious experience from symptoms of psychopathology. That is, I want to construe Abraham's devotion to sacrifice his son to God as being paralleled by our afflictions with command hallucinations. That is, this highly spiritual event in which Abraham is called to sacrifice his son as an act of devotion to God can be uncannily portrayed as an event that is similar to our struggles with the devastating "voices" that sometime command us.

My construal of Genesis 22:1-17 suggests that certain traditions within Genesis were familiar with the psychospiritual anomalies of command hallucinations. By extension, these traditions were also aware of the bizarre conversations that persons with untreated symptoms of psychotic illness can have with their "voices." I will contend that the dialogue between Abraham and God regarding Isaac's fate employs techniques of literary incription in which such bizarre conversations and command hallucinations are paradigmatic. My hunch is that these psycho
choliterary paradigms are essential to Genesis's efforts to de-legitimate a terrible social event: child sacrifice.

There is little question that some Palestinian religious cultures practiced the cultic acts of ritual child sacrifice, as indicated by various First Testament passages. For example, the problematic character of child sacrifice for the Hebrews is demonstrated in: Leviticus 20:2; Deuteronomy 12:30-31; Psalms 106:37-38; Jeremiah 7: 30-32; 19:3-5; and Ezekiel 16:20-21. I, therefore, offer that Abraham's flirtation with infanticide can be read against the backdrop of these various texts that explicitly treat the sinful forays of the Hebrew people into the domain of child sacrifice. It seems tenable that Hebraic religious sentiments and practices would be adversely "tested" by such local customs. Within that context, God's "test" of Abraham's religious devotion and loyalty can be read as a much larger "test" in which Hebraic religious culture must choose to condemn or condone the practice of child sacrifice. My reading of Genesis 22:1-17 suggests this cultic issue of child sacrifice was so important that only the paradigmatic incriptions of psychospiritual anomaly could suffice to render a definitive judgment.

Genesis 22:1 immediately establishes a psychospiritual context in which Abraham hears the "voice" of God, much like a person with un-treated psychosis might hear a "voice." Indeed, it is most unfortunate for many consumers that when they do hear command hallucinations, they immediately and implicitly believe with tenacious resolve that the "voice" is from God, or perhaps a demon. In verse 2 of this chapter, we can portray that the "voice" Abraham hears from God commanding him to sacrifice his son, Isaac, is similar to the sorts of command hal-lucinations that some consumers suffer.

Verses 3-6 are reminiscent of the tedious preoccupations some persons with severe mental illness experience. For Abraham's prepara-tion of the donkey, cutting wood for the offering, and carrying fire and knife seem to parallel the ponderous, tedious, psychotic obsessiveness that some persons with severe mental illness employ to carry out the tasks of their command hallucinations. We see that Abraham, much like persons with severe mental illness, experienced some confounding external obsessions with tedious and laborious actions as he prepared to offer his son, Isaac, as a burnt offering to God.

In verses 7 & 8, Isaac and Abraham converse about where the sacrificial animal awaits. Abraham's response to Isaac that God would provide a lamb is thematic at two levels. First, we can suggest that Abraham, much like a person with untreated psychosis, wants to hide his sinister intent from his son. Abraham's answer is reminiscent of some of our paranoia during the dramas of our command experiences--for we dare not disclose the sinister secrets that God or the demons demand we perform. For Abraham cannot openly and honestly inform Isaac that he is the intended burnt offering. After all, the announcement of (seemingly psychotic) secrets would warn Isaac of his danger and of his father's (apparent) insanity. Such a literary use of psycho-spiritual polemics does indeed parallel the secretive nature of psychotic distortions. For it is frequently characteristic that persons who dialogue with "voices' or hear command hallucinations will go to great lengths to conceal the true meanings of the "secret" messages brought to them by their "voices." After all, we dare not disclose our "secret" messages lest we be punished by God or the demons; or be labeled as crazy. Also, there are our own doubts whether we should obey the commands, for we surmise we might just be crazy. I see a parallel of these experiences in Abraham's hiding of this command secret as being of such personal, psychospiritual magnitude and distortion that he cannot trust this reality and his experience enough to disclose it honestly.

However, at a second level, Abraham's statement that God will provide a lamb for the sacrifice functions as a foundational event of psychospiritual foreshadowing. In this second level of our psychospiritual drama, we begin to hear the socio-theological pronouncement that child sacrifice is anathema, or cursed. Instead of practicing the insanity of child sacrifice, the patriarchal and paradigmatic figure of Abraham has announced God's judgment. Even as God provides a ram for the sacrifice and commands Abraham not to kill his son, so the Hebrew nation is not to practice the heinous, (psychotic) evil of ritual child sacrifice. I thus conjecture at a psychospiritual level Abraham's odyssey is used to de-legitimate practices of infanticide. Thus, we see the triumph of sanity, which chooses to forego such heinous evil.

The prohibition of child sacrifice is further legitimated in verses 15-17. Here, again, Abraham hears the "voice" of the angel; and once again, we may conjecture that Genesis employs such psychotic dialogue to de-legitimate child sacrifice. We are privileged to hear angelic "voices" function as a blessing to Abraham. For the angel promises that Abraham and his descendants will be blessed throughout human history--precisely because Abraham and his children have opted not to practice the evils of child sacrifice. A psychospiritual reading of Genesis 22 further construes that such "symptomatics" function as bedrock on which certain of the Abrahamic covenants are built.

Moreover, via this rendition of Genesis 22, Abraham can become an archetypal self object for those of us who suffer the devastating symptoms of mental illness. He has heard "voices" commanding him to kill, even as some consumers have. Like us, he struggled and fought the impulse to evil by choosing life for his son. As he triumphed and brought blessing to his descendants, perhaps we might find courage to fight, struggle and do the right thing. Perhaps this reading will give hope to those who fight commanding "voices"--consumers, families and treatment teams. Perhaps Abraham's experiences can be read as powerful beacons of hope for consumers and those who love us. For in this story about Abraham, sanity triumphs; and we know that sanity can triumph for many persons with untreated or mistreated severe mental illnesses who are the most likely to be afflicted by command hallucinations. Perhaps our society will find ways to employ more community-based treatments to minister to the untreated along with the near-miraculous, soul-restoring medications that are becoming available. Let us find hope in Abraham through whom God shows us that God chooses sanity for Her/His children.

At this juncture, let us turn our attention to the so-called conversion of Saul; and as we do let us tread the holy path of the Damascus Road with the Saint. As we do, though, it would be good to recall Anton Boisen's words and observations about Paul's conversion experience. Boisen was quick to point out that a purely clinical, psychodynamic analysis of the Saint's conversion would conclude that Paul certainly had mental illness. For the features of his conversion read much like the onset of paranoid schizophrenia: visual hallucinations, audible hallucinations, tactile hallucinations and delusional activity.

However, I believe Boisen was correct in his assessment that such purely clinical analyses would be completely reductionistic. Rather, for Boisen, the events of Saul's conversion constituted Paul as a religious genius. The central point we must recall from Boisen is the manner by which he ascribed religious experience to psychological distress. If a mental/psychological break resulted in health or progress in the formation of the personality that was afflicted--to that extent the sufferer's turmoil had religious bearing. However, if no good could be gleaned from the crisis, the experience lacked religious significance and should be treated in purely psychiatric or clinical terms. As it is somewhat dated, we must add to Boisen's view that health and recovery are more likely today due to incredible advances in treatment modalities, medical science, and medications.

Prior to changing his name to Paul, the Saint's given name was Saul- - Saul of Tarsus. Saul was a "Jew among Jews," proud of his Hebraic ancestry and devoted to the Jewish faith. Saul's fervor for Judaism is well attested to in the Second Testament. Both in Acts and in several of his epistles, Saul's fanatic devotion is well documented. For Saul, the Jew, had political and religious authority to have newly converted Christians stripped of their rights and even to be imprisoned. Saul was a fierce persecutor of the fledgling Christian churches and he was zealous in his devotion to and practice of persecution.

Acts 9:1-9; 18-19, recalls the details of Saul's' conversion. Ironically, Saul was traveling to Damascus to obtain legal and religious writs to imprison Christians in Jerusalem. The irony is that Saul's conversion occurred while he was sojourning in the performance of his commission to persecute the Christians. Then, on the road, as it were, the persecutor became the persecuted. Let us highlight the events (psychospiritual symptomatics) of Saul's conversion.

First, Acts tells us that Saul saw a bright light flash from heaven. Then while falling to the ground in panic and terror, Saul heard a voice, which asked him: "Saul, Saul, why do you persecute me?" Saul then begins to dialogue with the voice that told him, "I am Jesus, whom you are persecuting." Furthermore, Jesus tells Saul to go to Damascus, where he will receive further instruction. For three days, Acts notes, Saul was left blind and could not eat or drink. However, after a local Christian, Ananias, prayed with him, Paul experiences his final conversion--as scales fall from his eyes. Paul regains his sight and is enabled to eat and drink. Thereafter, Saul was known as Paul--his Christian name.

For now, let us review Paul's conversion as containing markers that are indicative of a mental health crisis. From a clinical standpoint, as though we have case study material at hand, we can read this passage as involving some sort of psychotic break. Paul had visual hallucinations--he saw a bright light flash so intensely that it blinded him. He had tactile hallucinations, as well. We note the report of blindness--a bodily anomaly; and we consider the report that scales fell from his eyes--another somatic feature. Paul then has audible hallucinations; and has a psychotic dialogue with a "voice" that he believes belongs to Jesus. The theme of this "conversation" also has symptomatic features. For, indeed, it is during this dialogue that Saul, the persecutor, becomes the persecuted. That is, we can construe Jesus' voice as functioning similarly to delusions of persecution in which Paul believes himself to be persecuted by Christ for having persecuted many helpless Christians. At the level of psychodynamic metaphor, the theme of persecution is striking. A psychodynamic reading of this thematic could suggest that Saul's "symptoms," crises, and "break" were the result of his own unresolved guilt and shame for persecuting helpless Christians--solely on the basis of their religious experience and practice. Such a reading could suggest that Saul's heart was breaking with compassion for those he harmed; and from his personal sense of self-loathing for having acted with inhuman zeal and fervor.

At this point, there is no dispute that Paul's Damascus Road conversion was a crisis. If we read the text solely as a clinical document, Paul suffered a definite psychotic episode. However, a psychospiritual reading of the text can take us through other diagnostic paths. Acts is very descript in casting Saul as a persecutor of the Church--well ahead and in advance of reporting his conversion. We know Saul is cast as being basically evil--the antithesis of the Church portrayed as its primary persecutor. I suggest that we read Saul's "symptoms" as metaphorically psychotic features of unresolved guilt, self-loathing and a desire to leave behind his past as a persecutor. Thus, Paul's events of conversion, or symptomatics, can be read as psychotic events that were germinated by deeply felt, unresolved, unrelenting psychospiritual turmoil. We can surmise that Paul's crisis and conversion are inseparable facets of psychospiritual experience. Yet, as a conversion experience we witness the hand of God moving in history.

We can say as much of the experiences of Abraham and Moses. Abraham's struggle with "voices" commanding him to kill his son was a definite crisis for both father and son. However, Abraham lived through the crisis to experience conversion. He was transformed by divine persuasion to recognize that God detests child sacrifice and that God would not ask him to sacrifice Isaac. Moses lived through crisis as well. In his search for identity and meaning in life, Moses encountered some psychospiritual anomalies--visual hallucinations, audio hallucinations, and dialogue with a "voice." Yet, these (psychospiritually) symptomatic experiences of Abraham, Moses and Paul are not the most important elements of these overall conversion crises.

Rather, let us suggest that crises are opportunities for conversion, opportunities for growth, and opportunities for transformation. Following Boisen, we see in these three conversion accounts that their crises were steps toward growth within a larger drama. Thus, the meaning of these psychospiritual experiences does not rest or rely on their facticity as being terrible, awful symptoms of psychosis to be dismissed by counsel and quieted by haldol. Because there is a fine line between religious experience and mental illness, I cannot dismiss these crises as being the pure phenomena of thought disorders.

"Crisis" is an interesting word. In English, as used in particular for stigmatic diagnostics, most persons and many mental health professionals (including pastoral counselors) regard mental health crises as anathema. Crises are regarded as bad things. Crises are to be avoided. Crises happen to "them" and not to "us;" for "we" are healthy, fit and sound, while "they" are infirm. Crises require catastrophic treatment. Crises, especially the sort of mental illness, are shameful and debasing, evidence of weakness, evidence of sin, and evidence of punishment for bad choices.

Although the vignettes of Moses, Abraham and Paul involve developmental and spiritual crises, there are other levels of Biblical tradition that view such crises in holistic terms. For we see in all of these stories that the crises, experiences and symptoms are not devastating ends in and of themselves. They occur within the context of life-changing, life-altering conversion. For operative within these Biblical texts are ancient views of crisis, which are lost to most of us. In the Bible, crises are opportunities. Crises are events for self-assessment; for judgment; for decision-making, to plan, amend, or create anew; times to "take stock," or evaluate one's life and choices. As such, crises are primarily opportunities to grow, develop, change, become healthier and stronger, to re-orient one's stance to life's issues. For crises represent the human's ability to make meaning of and give meaning to psychospiritual anomalies within the context of healthy conversion and transformation. Indeed, in his book, *Stages of Faith,* James Fowler makes the seminal point that such crises are actually the nodal points that germinate transition from one faith stage to another. Given such analyses, perhaps religious persons and groups might esteem our difficulties as crises, which can become points for holistic conversion, growth, development and deepened faith. Perhaps more mental health professionals, families and faith groups will come to recognize that recovery with severe mental illness is possible with effective medications, counseling, more assertive community treatment and interventions, and the faith or spiritual trust that many consumers hold dear.

The last vignette I wish to portray in this chapter is one in which Jesus heals a "demon-possessed" man. I have placed "demon-possessed" in quotes because I intend to replace it with phrases such as "a person with mental illness," or "a man with severe mental illness," etc. My effort here is to convey my sense that we are not dealing with demon possession, but with ancient, archaic, although Biblical, descriptions of persons who suffered from the ravages of untreated, severe mental illness. This Second Testament healing/conversion story occurs in the three synoptic Gospels: Matthew 8:28-34; Mark 5:1-20; and Luke 8:26-39. The portrayal I will sketch borrows liberally from each Gospel's account. My hope is to draw out from each description various features and indicators that render the afflicted soul in these narratives as being a person who lived with untreated, severe mental illness.

The locale of this story's action is in the region of Samaria. The importance of this observation becomes clear as we remember and consider that Samaritans were deeply despised by the Jews of Jesus' day. Samaritans were regarded as "unclean," which meant any Jew who came into contact with a Samaritan became "unclean" him/herself. The result of which was that the now "unclean" Jew had to undergo stringent socio-religious purifications to re-enter Jewish society. Otherwise, an "unclean" person was a social outcast. "Strike one" for our person with untreated mental illness was that he was a Samaritan and, therefore, "unclean" by virtue of race and ethnicity. "Strike two" for this unfortunate soul was that he had mental illness, which in itself rendered him "unclean" by virtue of disease. For here let us recall that the man is said to have an "*unclean* spirit." Both "conditions" rendered him "unclean" and ritually impure to the Jewish-Christian audiences whom heard and read these stories.

Disgracefully, this man with severe mental illness had no place to call home, other than the graveyard he "haunted." By the way, contact with the dead also made a person "unclean"--"strike three" for our unfortunate. A modern parallel might be the stigmatized plight of our nation's homeless persons, of whom some demographers estimate that one-third of such sufferers have untreated, severe and persistent mental illnesses. If this is accurate, we can surmise that our hero stunk, talked or mumbled to himself, ate infrequently, and was subject to a much-shortened life-expectance. Well, the three Gospels agree that this man had been chained to the graves with shackles and fetters. But even then he could not be contained, as he would always, eventually, break his bonds. Too bad, however, that "modern" chemical and physical restraints render it virtually impossible for a consumer to escape when "chained" for "treatment." While we might find it repugnant (or refreshing) that our hero could extricate himself, his plight did not improve. For his condition was so severe that, once liberated from chains, he would beat himself with rocks and the broken chains themselves. We further read that his condition was so tormenting that his habit was to cry out and howl in anguish and unrelieved suffering.

As I have mentioned previously, my personal opinion is that our hero was not demon-possessed, but suffered from untreated, severe mental illness. However, I believe I can certify with some degree of precision that this narrative reads like the "treatment" many consumers suffered through while confined to psych hospitals, asylums, aboard the "ships of fools," or during the "witch hunts." For hundreds, if not thousands of years, it has been customary to chain, restrain and shackle persons with severe mental illnesses. That our afflicted soul lived in a graveyard indicates his lowest status in society. For he could live nowhere in his village except on the outskirts of civilization as a despised outcast. It's interesting to note that many, if not all of America's old psychiatric hospitals were segregated from towns, cities and the "chronically normal" by many miles of distance and ostracism.

Our afflicted hero also demonstrates severe symptoms of self-harm and self-mutilation. Quite often, persons with untreated mental illness can be very self-destructive; and that is the case here, as it has been mentioned that our unfortunate beat himself with rocks. I also find the man's dialogue with Jesus to be most telling. When people with severe mental illnesses first enter treatment, and even long into treatment, there is an incredible tendency not to trust one's treatment team enough to disclose the character, intensity, severity and pervasiveness of our symptoms. It is even harder for completely unmedicated souls to divulge symptoms, who need treatment but refuse, reject or are denied treatment by stigma and law. Such mistrust is part of the course of our illnesses and renders it very hard to trust providers or treatment teams, whom we might regard as being the most loathsome of enemies. Our deeply troubled hero is no exception to this phenomenon. For he begs Jesus, "...do not torment me." It is a sad commentary that we find it so hard to trust those whom would help us. But such is the nature of our symptoms, especially when they are untreated. But such is also the case of our experience of being treated as "unclean" by the prejudicial stigma with which most members of our culture disenfranchise and despise us.

As the narrative proceeds, the man with mental illness notices a large herd of pigs grazing on a hillside. Interestingly, our hero asks Jesus to send the "*unclean* spirits" into this herd of swine. When Jesus consents, our hero is a victim no more and is cured when the "unclean spirits" enter the herd of swine. Economically unfortunate for the townspeople and herders, we are told that all the swine rush down a hillside and jump off the cliffs to drown in the nearby sea. Later on the curious villagers inspect the once-deeply troubled man and see him "clothed and in his right mind." Upon seeing the man healed and knowing that the pigs were dead and drowned the villagers are horrified and demand that Jesus and the disciples leave the district immediately.

In a nutshell, one aspect of my interpretation of these narratives can be boiled down to the sentiment that despite God's (healing) efforts to be in solidarity with persons who have severe mental illnesses, society seeks to thwart this healing. For in this story, Jesus' cure of our hero's mental illness is an act of solidarity between divine flesh and despised, "unclean" flesh. That society thwarts, does not understand recovery, or refuses to celebrate God's desire to be with us, let me explain. For here we will explore the dynamics of "uncleanliness"--stigmatizing prejudice and unholy disdain.

The location of this story is, once again, a Samaritan village. The narrative was told to Jewish -Christian audiences; and these people still were influenced by their own unholy, stigmatic opinions. As we have presented, the Samaritans themselves were regarded as "unclean." In fact, the implicit, symbolic logic of these narratives renders the Samaritans as being equal to the pigs, and, therefore, as "unclean." Consider for a moment that the dietary and socio-religious customs of Jews rendered swine as "unclean." Hence, Jews would not raise swine, touch swine, let alone eat swine--for pigs were an unholy abomination to the socio-religious conscience of the Jews. Things get worse. Coming into physical contact with a pig rendered a Jew "unclean"--which meant the "unclean" person was shunned, outcast and rejected by society until s/he could be ritually purified.

Unfortunately, our hero with mental illness was "unclean." The litany of stigmatized uncleanliness reads as follows: Samaritans are "unclean;" swine are "unclean;" persons with mental illness are "unclean." A devastatingly haunting equation thus emerges: Samaritans are swine, as are persons with mental illness. Essentially, our stigmatically victimized hero is an "unclean" pig.

Given such dismal dynamics, our story becomes a narrative of culture's corruptive subversion and society's tendencies to resist God's desires for change and healthy conversion. Although through the healing actions of Jesus God has subverted a physical and stigmatized illness, culture's corruptions seek to subvert that which can be good, healthy and wholesome. For Jesus entered into solidarity with our afflicted hero. However, despite being healed to the point of being "clothed and in his right mind," our hero's neighbors still despised him--for they equated the essence of his afflictions (mental illness) as equal to the unholy and "unclean" character of loathsome swine. At one level, then, we see that this healing/conversion story tackles the problem of how individuals and societies tend to resist goodness and healing due to prejudice and stigma. For this tale carries the somber thematics of ancient, deeply held prejudices that persist to the present, regarding persons with severe mental illness as worthless, unholy pigs who deserve to be chained up, restrained, left in graveyards, homeless, untreated and abandoned by society. Perhaps this story tells us that although God's desire is to bring health and wholeness to as many of the afflicted as possible, society remains hard to convert to habits and practices that can inspire restored meaning and holistic life.

God is the great companion--the fellow-sufferer who understands. Alfred North Whitehead

The mentally ill are like us, only more.
Chaplain Paul Tomlinson, SEH.

Chapter 5
Jesus: Like Us, Only More
(Solidarity as Clinical Theodicy)

As a Chaplain Intern in the Clinical Pastoral Education program at St. Elizabeths Hospital, I had the privilege to attend the lectures of Chaplain Paul Tomlinson. One afternoon Chaplain Tomlinson declared, "The mentally ill are like us, only more." As he spoke these words my soul twitched with excitement and expectation. But I did not yet know why.

Now, I do. As the Chaplain elaborated on his theme, I felt afresh the hope that moments of solidarity bring. The words, "like us, only more" awoke a sense of kinship, of connection, or reconciliation between my alienated mentally ill self and the world of "chronic normals." The hope I felt in that gracious moment was an event of solidarity.

Solidarity.

Chaplain Tomlinson's lecture ministered healthfully to me. He asked us, his students, to experience our worlds and the worlds of persons with severe mental illnesses. I ask you, now, to do the same. He asked us to recall and consider a moment when we had felt sad. Perhaps in our young lives we had experienced the pangs of sorrow and sadness that accompany the grief of bereavement. Perhaps we had felt overwhelmed with disappointing sadness when we had to break up and break off our relationship with a first love. He invited us to feel those sorrows again, anew, afresh. Then he brought us back to the present and our sadness was gone, just another faded memory. We were invited to consider that persons with major depression feel such sadness and sorrows, too. He asked us to try to imagine what it might feel like to experience the abyss of the complete loss of pleasure--that never goes away and is unrelenting. He asked us to try to experience the sadness a person with depression feels from sun-up to sundown, which requires no cause and does not stop. He asked us to attempt to feel the utter despair of a worthless, empty, meaningless life trying to end its pain-- by committing suicide. Imagine a despairing sadness that has no end; except when you're asleep. The mentally ill are like us, only more.

Next we were invited to remember a moment of magical happiness, a moment of exuberant joy, or pleasure fulfilled. Maybe we could re- member the intense pride and happiness of getting our first "A" in our toughest class. Perhaps we had felt the awesome excitement of being a starting member on one of the state's best high school basketball teams.

Then, we remembered the deep joy and fulfillment felt at the moment of a first child's birth. Well, the Chaplain told us that persons with bipolar illness also have such wonderful moments of pleasure. But during a manic phase, the euphoric "high" seems endless. For some, these are days, even weeks, of incredibly productive and enjoyable artistic or intellectual achievement. For others, the "high" takes on psychotic dimensions as they silently laugh at having successfully hidden their divine status. But for some persons who live through mania the energy that never ends is agitated, irritable, anti-social and maybe even belligerent. Yet manic moods never last. They come to an end; and when they do, one falls to the earth in a dreadful crash. For the other side in bipolar illness is unanticipated and unexpected depression. But it can be a dark depression that lasts for days, weeks, or seemingly unending months. Instead of laughter, there are weeping tears and weeping hearts. Instead of increased productivity, there is the absolute inability to function. Yet, unlike the ups and downs that "normals" have, which end and are forgotten, the manias and depressions of bipolar illness do not end. They just continue to cycle, in and out, up and down, happy then sad, awake but asleep. The mentally ill are like us, only more.

Then there is schizophrenia; the cancerous death sentence of the mental illnesses.

Try to recall a moment when you were absolutely terrified. Perhaps the neighborhood bully was about to victimize you again with taunt and fist. Get in touch with your pounding heart, your body trembling from the overdose of adrenalin and cortisol that rip through your muscles. These are moments of horror, moments of "fight or flight." But, suddenly, the bully's Mom calls him home to dinner, and you have been saved. Your fears subside, the terrors are forgotten and your body relaxes.

Or consider a time when you were the center of public attention. Everybody was talking about just how lovely and sensationally stunning your new dress was that night. The topic of locker room chatter was about your awesome dunk in last night's winning game (which also made the front page in your hometown newspaper). Maybe you were the "talk of the town" because you and your date were the first interracial couple to attend the Prom--ever! Perhaps, though, you caught the coach's wrath and scorn for an entire week--just because your lousy defense lost the game. But soon enough, the "buzz" stops and you slip back into the normalcies of being just another "average Jo(e)."

When was the last time you were watching TV and you listened to that same old commercial? Somehow, that ad has a magical way of reminding you tax season is an excellent time to buy a new car. One might say the ad "prompted" or "reminded" you of an important task or goal you had. Better yet, when was the last time the pastor's sermon really "spoke" to you, gave you a "message" or a "word from God" that breathed life back into your heart? Yet, such moments of serendipitous clairvoyance are rare, momentary and soon forgotten.

But for a person with active symptoms of paranoid schizophrenia, the terror never ends. The adrenalin, the anxiety and the tension do not subside; because the only condition you are capable of is "fight or flight."

For no reason. Every waking hour of each unmercifully untreated day is a mind-blowing, body-ripping struggle with sheer terror...terror that does not go away, terror that has no cause other than neuropathology. The mentally ill are like us, only more. Then there are those pesky "voices." At first they might be nice and flatteringly grandiose; and being the center of their unceasing praise and adoring attentions is glorious. But, later on...they get mean...even destructive. They start screaming when you wake up. They command you to kill your self, to hit your brother, to run away from home, or to bow down to the postman in homage. If you don't obey them and don't do as they command, they punish you. They call you "Ugly." "Worthless." "Disgustingly fat and creepy." Maybe they even tell you that you are "Anti-Christ, evil and sinful." You can never escape from these "mumbles." You can never be anything other than the center of their unwelcome and unsolicited attentions. The mentally ill are like us, only more. Yet, let's not forget the TV, the radio, a magazine or favorite newspaper. As you listen to the media, you begin to discern the embedded secret codes that are intended only for you. But if you tell anyone that the TV sends you secret messages, you know you will be called crazy; and you could even be punished. Reading. Reading has become a meaningless exercise in futile absurdity. You stare at the same sentence, the same paragraph, or the same page for hours--seeking to decipher their hidden meanings within the jumbles of discontinuity and incongruity. All communication is absurd. The mentally ill are like us, only more.

Like us, only more. The ring of these scenarios resounded through my heart in the compassion they conveyed. The word "solidarity" suddenly ceased being a cognitive referent limited to an objective analysis of what socialists are supposed to have and do. Rather, solidarity has become for me the summation of pragmatic processes and experiences of loving and being loved. Solidarity is about the heart-felt emotions that accompany one person's efforts to understand and comfort another's pains. Solidarity is the joyous task of "being-with" another soul who simply needs you to "be-there." Solidarity is a gracious moment when permission is given to trusted, beloved others who wish to "be-with" me in moments of need. Like us, only more.

I have a friend who is like me, only more. Well, he's more like a role model or mentor. He inspires me, gives me hope, keeps me struggling and gives me courage to fight, strive, thrive and survive. Sounds like a pretty good counselor; or what a good counselor could be like. But I'm referring to Jesus, of course.

In what follows, I have as a goal to advocate for some rather unorthodox readings of various New Testament texts and tradition. I will render these stories to portray a Jesus who is like us, only more. By demonstrating that Jesus is like us, only more, I hope to uncover a Christ who is in solidarity with persons who suffer with severe mental illness. Jesus' solidarity with persons who have mental illness is a strikingly important sentiment. For if God's Son can be shown to have been personally intimate with experiences similar to our psychopathologies, there emerges a powerful sense of hope for consumers. Perhaps, we too, can survive the traumas of our pathologies, just as Jesus endured similar conundrums as our companion in solidarity.

It becomes important therein to detail what it means for the Son of God to be a companion in solidarity with consumers. The outcome sought in this endeavor is an outline of features of a clinical theodicy based on God's solidarity with us. The first task will be to promote a psychospiritual reading of some New Testament texts that concretely establish Jesus as Emmanuel--God with us. The second task will be to show how God's solidarity with us can generate hope for consumers to endure the genuine evils of severe mental illness.

Matthew's Gospel uniquely names Jesus as Emmanuel, which means "God is with us." There in the 23rd verse of Matthew's first chapter, the evangelist establishes that Jesus' importance, identity, and ministries are matters of solidarity--"being-with-us." An earthy reading of Jesus' birth is a fine place to start.

I have to admit that up until a few years ago, my understanding of the Synoptic Gospels' birth narratives was very naive. I had no idea what a manger was. I knew from the song that Jesus was laid in a manger, but I thought this manger was synonymous with the word "barn." To my mind, Jesus' manger was just a quaint, rustic, comfortable barn.

While attending New Year's Mass with a friend, though, I finally learned what the manger was. It's actually the little food trough animals eat out of when they're feeding in a barn. The priest further defined this manger by pointing out that its function was to keep food clean from and uncontaminated by barnyard filth.

Immediately, my imagination started reconfiguring some naive conceptions of the manger scenarios. All of a sudden the bright Christmas card halos around Jesus', Joseph's and Mary's heads went dark. All of a sudden I transposed my grandfather's barn into the biblical images of Jesus' birth. Grampa's barn was old, rickety, and dark. In the summer it stank to high heaven from its decaying compost of rotting food, straw and excrement on the ground. At its best it was hot, steamy and oppressive. In the winter, his barn was damp, muddy, drafty, moldy, dark and strewn like a fecal minefield. All of a sudden it became highly probable and somewhat plausible that Jesus was born in a nasty old barn, sort of like Grampa's.

How incredible it is to imagine that Emmanuel started being-with-us by being-born-in-muck. From the outset, Jesus' solidarity with us begins in the muckish filth of a dingy, damp, drafty barn. The message is clear. God shows us S/He is with us not by being above the sheep dip of our trials and traumas; but by entering our world through the muckish reek of a barn. In solidarity with us, Christ is born into the same sort of filthy crap that consumers face every day--stigma, discrimination, economic poverty, social ostracism and ridicule.

In my Spiritual Skills Group at the Adult & Child (mental health) Center, I have encouraged my clients to imagine how they would feel knowing they started life being born in the muckish filth of a barn. Quite reasonably, we all felt the shame and dishonor of such ignoble beginnings. Yet, when we started to consider that Jesus had such a crappy start, our familiarity with life's absurd filth became a bit more tolerable. My clients were able to connect with the depiction of a Christ who was intimately familiar with the sheep dip life had thrown at them. All of a sudden, the inaccessibility of a haloed infant was replaced and transformed by an accessible little tike who started his life in a pile of muckish filth, much like the reekish crap that accompanies the destructive degenerations during the onset of severe mental illness. Somehow, feeling that Jesus had survived such ignobility helps us strive not to stay stuck in our muck.

An inspiring echo of such divine solidarity rings through the verses of the Christ-hymn in Chapter 2 of Philippians. This hymn is a theological archetype, which prioritizes divine solidarity with broken humanity. This hymn communicates the sentiment of solidarity that is born when God comes to be-with-us. In this hymn, the "most high" becomes the "most nigh." Herein, Jesus is portrayed as trading the mantle of divinity for the scourge of human slavery--a sentence of death. Imagine that, trading power for powerlessness; trading hope for hopelessness; trading eternity for death; trading the golden halls of heaven for the crap-encrusted stench of earth. Through such images we can begin to see that Jesus is very much like us.

Another moment in the uncovering of divine solidarity is an alternative rendition of Matthew and Mark's account of Jesus' baptism and desert trials. In the tradition I grew up with, these passages are generally depicted as being serenely genteel and devoid of any real or meaningful struggle. But the reading I intend to offer marks a violent episode in the tale of God's solidarity with us. To guide this construal, I reassert a significant presupposition: There is a fine line between the mnemonic details of Jesus' spiritual experience and the elements of symptomatic psychopathology experienced by persons with severe mental illnesses. God's solidarity with us rests on a meaningful construal of the biblical pictures of Jesus' baptism and desert trials.

My reading of Mark 1:10 relies on the confluence of some Greek definitions, scriptural tradition and blind chance. When Jesus comes up from the baptismal waters of the Jordan River, Mark's Jesus sees the "heavens torn apart." Whereas, Matthew's Jesus witnesses the "heavens opened to him." I prefer the violence of Mark's memory to the gentle civility of Matthew's. I do so following the translation of commentator Lamar Williamson, who understands that in Mark the heavens are actually "being ripped apart" (Williamson, p. 34). It seems obvious that watching the skies rip apart is a much more violent event than one of the heavens merely opening.

It seems that a "gentle" reading of Jesus' baptism hinges on another serene image--that of the Holy Spirit descending gently, peacefully, tenderly and affirmingly, like a nice, softly floating dove. But I would like to advance a violently de/constructive construal of the dove's activity, based on happenstance. Several years ago, while visiting at a friend's home, a pet bird escaped from its cage and started flying through the house. Unaccustomed to its shrill chirps and dizzying dive-bomber passes, I panicked, felt scared and became disoriented. I was traumatized by its antics and was scared I might get bit by it or scratched by its talons. Thereafter, I prefer to infuse the possibility that Jesus, too, was terrified and traumatized by the overwhelming spirit of a wild bird descending upon the scene of his baptism. After all, it seems plausible that a wildly spirited bird might fly flashing from a heaven that had just been ripped apart. Let us now enter the temptation scenarios with such conviction.

First of all, Edward Schweizer's view of the desert trials renders Jesus as being "driven" into the wilds for a confrontational and violent struggle. Schweizer sees God's Spirit forcefully, almost coercively over-powering Jesus to the extent he had no other choice than to enter the wastelands. Schweizer depicts these trials as a battle with the forces of evil--a battle that cannot evaded (Schweizer, p. 42). Quite like us, Jesus has to face up to and deal with the evils and struggles that confront his existence. Now on this matter of being "driven" into the wilds, Williamson concurs that God is depicted as driving/forcing/herding Jesus into the fray. Yet, Williamson adds a further clarification, which enhances my violently de/constructive construal of the desert trials. Namely, he points out that this wilderness setting functions as a locale in which forces hostile to God dwell (Williamson, p. 36). Though these forces threaten to undercut Jesus' life, identity and ministry, Jesus does not choose to evade them. Rather, he opts to face these conflicts, struggles and evils; such, that without confronting these perils one might surmise that Jesus' life, identity and ministry would have been irrevocably altered, diminished and forever changed.

Like us, only more. Persons with severe mental illness might use a wilderness metaphor to depict the arena in which we struggle daily with forces that are definitely hostile to our lives, our identities and our vocations. Certainly the disruptions of magical thinking, self-harm and grandiosity to which we are prone create within us destitute and barren souls. Most definitely such violent struggles with evil redefine who we are, who we might become and how we choose to exist. It is with similar understandings that we turn to examine Matthew.

Matthew 4:1-11 can be read as an amplification of Mark's recollections of Jesus' struggles and conflicts in the desert. It can also be read as a narrative in which predetermined outcomes are not guaranteed. Indeed, the very essence of Jesus' life, identity and ministry hang in the balance of how these struggles are resolved--much like how the lives of persons with severe mental illness hinge upon our daily struggles with evil. After Jesus has not eaten for forty days, Satan comes to tempt Him in the wastelands; the minimal essence of which is a profound identity crisis. This crisis can be construed further as depiction of a sort of deprivation dementia resulting from malnutrition and prolonged exposure to the hostile elements of a desert. Or, even further, this crisis can be viewed as another example of the premise that asserts there is a fine line between religious experience and psychopathology. In sum, after being forced by God into the desert to fight, Jesus's choice to enter the barrens leads to an identity crisis following the deprivations of having not eaten for forty days.

From a psychospiritual perspective, the following three temptations with which Jesus contends can be read as religious counterparts to some of the symptoms of severe mental illness. The temptation to turn stone to bread sounds much like a flirtation with the magical thinking we sometimes experience. It's a type of irrationality in which we might magically view others or ourselves as having special gifts or powers that enable, for example, the transmutation of matter. When examined as a moment of deprivation dementia, this temptation makes incredible sense as an instinct to survive prolonged battle, struggle and malnutrition in a hostile environment. Jesus is like us, only more.

The temptation to throw himself down from the cliffs also has a counterpart in symptoms of severe mental illness. Often times, consumers with a variety of different diagnoses struggle with thoughts of self-harm. These thoughts can manifest as habitual cutting on oneself; as habitual starvation of oneself; or as thoughts and attempts of suicide, just to name a few. Certainly a temptation to end one's life makes sense as a plausible, though ill advised solution to forty days' exposure to hostile elements without food. Perhaps Jesus is like us, only more.

The last temptation is recorded as an offer from Satan for Jesus to rule the world. If I walked into my psychiatrist's office and told her that Russian diplomats had revealed my identity as a Romanov survivor, I think her brow might rise in concerned suspicion. If I further told her I would soon be assuming the imperial throne of Russia, I think she would assess I was actively psychotic. Specifically, she most likely would have diagnosed me as experiencing delusions of grandeur. It seems plausible then, from a psychospiritual point of view that Jesus might have been familiar with personal notions of grandiosity. Again, Jesus is like us, only more.

Are not the identity crises of persons with severe mental illnesses akin to Jesus' struggles? Our crises tend to occur in isolation, in seclusion, deep within the deserts of meaningful life stripped away. Some of us think magically when we believe we possess powers to inflict great catastrophe or create great good. Also, thoughts and actions of self-harm, self-mutilation and suicide are common in our crises. For it is not uncommon to wish oneself dead, rather than face the daily struggles and evil phantasms of severe mental illness. Oh, how we pine for a moment of grandiose or expansive mood. How nice it would be to live as the imperial monarch of earth, or another star system, just the same!

Jesus is like us, only more. He was born in the muckish reek of a nasty barn. But he did not stay stuck in that muck. Swayed and influenced by powers and forces he likely did not understand, Jesus lived through the wasteland struggles of certain identity crisis. He is portrayed as having been confronted by the unnerving chaos of magical thinking, thoughts of self-harm and expansions of grandiosity. Such a Christ is indeed very much like us; but is also a role model and master beyond us. For he, too, found ways to survive and thrive beyond the evils that threatened to destroy his life, his identity and his ministry. Perhaps the Christ who is like us can serve to call us forward, to continue struggling to survive the evils we face, and to work anew each day to extricate our lives from the muckish reeks in which we live.

For most consumers, the issue of medication compliance is very problematic. In our periods of denial, reinforced by stigma and the symptomatic course of our illnesses, we believe meds are not needed and we generally resist taking them. After all, who wants to think of themselves as being a "whacko" who needs psychotropic medications? Accordingly, it sometimes takes years before a consumer can finally realize, accept and understand that recovery is entirely impossible without the powerful medications s/he needs. Furthermore, sometimes in our recovery processes, there have been moments when many of us wondered whether we're cured and therefore no longer need our medications. As a mental health chaplain, as a mental health advocate, as a case manager, and as a consumer myself, the issue of medication compliance is a matter of paramount importance. As a clinician interested in psychospiritual wholeness, I have long sought Biblical stories that convey to consumers "medications are OK," and that they are means God can use "to restore our souls." That is, I have searched long and hard to find a way to communicate Biblically that medications grant and restore life in ways that are ordained by God.

Such Biblical grounds are extremely important when we consider the psychospiritual conundrums that disable untreated consumers. For many of us have long histories of personal faith and spirituality, which continue into our lives with untreated illness. Unfortunately, institutional faith and symptomatics sometimes combine to reinforce our resistance to medication. We wonder why we need medication at all. For many of us have honestly felt that our need for psychotropic medication goes against the will of God and the healing power of the Holy Spirit. We reason that if we were truly persons of faith then God would somehow be enabled to heal us miraculously, without the need for any medication, ever. It becomes a lack of faith to need medication; and sometimes our magical thinking combines with our spirituality to reinforce our initial resistance to taking prescribed medications by making us believe that medications are actually evil. Or we might believe that our (symptomatic) problems are primarily spiritual, such that we don't have physical problems (neuropathology) that medication can alleviate. My first clinical attempts to use Biblical and theological interventions to normalize the need for medication were to suggest to my resistant clients that medications are sacramental like the elements of communion. I tried many times to suggest to my clients that medications are like the elements of communion, being elements of grace and goodness that could bring health and hope. But, generally, these interventions were not convincing and most of my clients remained skeptical.

After several unsuccessful attempts to inspire medication compliance via the metaphor of communion I somehow recalled an old Scriptural debate. Hence, I have turned to the Gospels recalling that there seems to have been a medical debate lodged within them. This debate revolves around the historical, theological and psychospiritual question whether Jesus was medicated or anesthetized during the crucifixion. Obviously, most seminarians know there was significant division amongst proto-Christians concerning the exact christological meaning of the sensibility that Jesus was fully human and fully divine. My contention here is that some of these divisions were characterized in part by how each Gospel treated the issue of Jesus drinking wine during the crucifixion.

My reading of these passages has important, consequential implications for persons with severe mental illness who need powerful psychotropic medications. Again, I will suggest that Jesus is like us, only more. In fact, as remembered and portrayed in the Johannine tradition, Jesus is so like us that he actually asked to be anesthetized by taking medicinal wine. If it can be demonstrated with plausibility that Jesus took medicine--in the guise of mixed wine--how much more permissible it is for consumers to take the psychotropic medications we need--without shame, without traumas of faith, without excuse and with hope. If the Johannine Christ can be shown to have needed medication, it might become a bit more "OK" for consumers to take medicine. The need for such christological hope is immense. Because of stigma, side effects and the course of severe mental illnesses themselves, all of us have questioned or denied our need for medical treatments and interventions at one time or another.

Our first step is to recognize the obvious. All four Gospels record there was some connection between Jesus and wine during his crucifixion (Cf., Mathew 27:34; Mark 15:23; Luke 23:36-38; and John 19:28). Consider also that in antiquity wine mixed with myrrh or gall was used as a drug. Such "sour" wine was used commonly during Roman crucifixions to anesthetize and alleviate some of the victim's suffering, pain and agony. It appears plausible the Gospels' debate involves controversy concerning the use of such an anesthetic potion during Jesus' crucifixion (Ross, *Interpreter's Dictionary of the Bible,* p. 850).

Now the Synoptics are in complete agreement that the Roman soldiers offered Jesus some sort of wine. In Matthew, it was wine mixed with gall. In Mark, it was wine mixed with myrrh. Luke states that it was "sour wine." Matthew reports that Jesus actually tasted the drink, but that he also spat it out. More cryptically, Mark states Jesus, "did not take" this mixture. Luke, alone in the synoptic traditions, locates the offer of sour wine within the context of soldiers mocking Jesus--daring him to save himself, as it were. Interestingly Luke makes no declaration whether Jesus tasted the wine, left it alone or spat it out.

My personal sense for these texts involves both Matthew's and Luke's pejorative views of Jesus needing medicinal wine. Matthew's narrative brings to mind an image of a "tough guy" who, when he tastes medicated wine, spits it out, because God's "tough guy" does not need medical help. By implication, Matthew's Christ totally rejects the need for any anesthetic during the crucifixion. Luke's sentiment is equally caustic. Luke uses the device of critical mockery to negate the value of medicated wine for Jesus' pain. One has the sense that part of the significance of Luke's text resides in its mocking critique that a Christ who needed to take medicated wine would be a Christ who implicitly mocks the self-sufficient power of the divine by taking the mixed potion.

However, the reading of John's Gospel that I submit is one I believe to be a treasure-trove for afflicted persons who need medical care. Only in John does Jesus ask for something to drink. John's portrayal has

Jesus declare, "*I am* thirsty," in expectation that his need for satiation would be met. John notes that some wine, a medical concoction in my opinion, was available. Unique to John is the recollection that Jesus actually welcomed, received and drank this medicinal wine. Interestingly, though, only after "receiving" this wine is Jesus able to declare, "It is finished." One has the sense that Jesus' acceptance of this (medicinal) "cup" is the final draught from, "...the cup that the Father has given me" (John 18:11).

I begin the process of completing this chapter by highlighting the features of what I call a clinical theodicy. At an intellectual level, the problems of theodicy constitute what are perhaps the greatest challenges to the integrity and coherence of Christian faith. The problems of how to reconcile genuine evils within nature and human experience with claims that God is all-loving and all-powerful constitute dilemmas that perplex faith and reason. At a clinical level, struggling with how one reconciles one's faith with the lived experience of disabling evil is perhaps the greatest psychospiritual challenge with which an afflicted soul must deal to become whole.

There are basically three alternative solutions to the intellectual enigmas of theodicy: classical theodicies; so-called character-building theodicies; and process theodicies. Each of these perspectives attempts to account for how a loving, powerful God remains worthy of our faith and worship in the face of the stark realities of genuine evil. However satisfying and inviting each of these solutions might be at an intellectual level, I find each of them to be rather inaccessible to the real victims of evil--precisely because they are cognitive solutions, fashioned outside the domain of clinical practice and need.

I thus locate the need for a clinical theodicy of solidarity within the real world needs and confines of clinically felt and experienced pain. The clinical theodicy I propose does not seek to explain evil or postulate how and why God permits evil. But it does seek to instill a hopeful sense of solidarity that is performative, pragmatic and experiential. I take this position due to the sensibility that the question of evil and God's relation to it is ultimately unanswerable. I believe that all answers to the question why or how it is that a world created good by a so-called, all-powerful, all-loving God includes genuine evil are ultimately provisional and partial. It seems much more clinically indicated, pragmatic and helpful to admit to suffering souls that I am just as perplexed as they are why there is evil and why they are confronted by it. What is clinically realistic, worthy and appropriate, though, is to offer unending solidarity; to offer unwavering support; to offer everlasting empathy and commiseration; or to offer the compassion of unconditional positive regard.

The pragmatics of clinical theodicy thus reside in the specific events and experiences of solidarity that assure the afflicted soul the trusted other will always be there to offer support and solace (e.g., recall the nature of self objects). Clinical theodicy enables a troubled heart to reduce and minimize the traumas of pathology, while it instills courage, vigor, hope and the will to live and endure--through the clinical intervention of therapeutic solidarity.

Solidarity as clinical theodicy conveys pragmatic, experiential hope to foster recovery-enhancing skills. In one sense, clinical relationships are most therapeutic when solidarity is experienced, lived and felt by both clinician and client. At another level, interactions of peer solidarity between consumers can generate hope through genuine commiserations of lived and felt empathy. In terms of psychospiriitual health, the experiences of endurance, hope and satiation emerge from God's solidarity with us.

The rendering of Jesus as like us (human), only more (divine), locates God's solidarity with suffering consumers through the lived moment of experiencing God-with-us. The old song echoes a moment of solidarity, as, "Nobody knows the troubles I've seen...nobody knows but Jesus." The Jesus I deem worthy of worshipping, following and emulating is the Christ who has been called to (help us to) cope with and survive the very pathologies that haunt other consumers and myself. God's solidarity with us is felt in the sentiment that God is not above us, as immune to and unaffected by our sorrows and symptoms. Rather, God's solidarity with us is a pragmatic, experiential promise from God resident in Christ. In and through Christ, God shows us S/He will never ask from us that which S/He does not expect or demand from Him/Herself. That which humans face as evil, God requires of Godself. Whatever path we trod, God will always be-with-us--feeling the same pain, experiencing similar pathologies and always inviting us to become more than who we already are, in each moment. Rather than being said to exist above and beyond our crappy, reekish experiences, God shows

Her/Himself to be in solidarity with us by honoring us with the presence of a Child who had to start life in the reekish muck of a barn. Far from being unaffected by the diseased pangs of our magical thinking, thoughts of self-harm and tendencies toward grandiosity, the Christ of divine solidarity demonstrates that God-is-with-us by experiencing our misfortunes in his desert crises. Instead of being left alone to take our medicine in shame, we have a role model in the thirsts of the Crucified One who cried for medical help. Indeed, on the cross, the Healer became the Healed.

GLOSSARY

ACT Team Assertive Community Treatment Teams provide mental health treatment services aggressively with community-based interventions. ACT Teams work in the community and in consumers' homes rather than waiting for consumers to come to the mental health centers for treatment. ACT Teams are multi-disciplinary units comprised of a prescriber, psychiatric nurses, case managers, supported employment specialists, addictions specialists, peer support specialists, and a team leader.

Aletheia Is a Greek word for truth that was a central feature of Martin Heidegger's analysis of Being. Heidegger defined truth as a matter of unconcealment or disclosure.

American Pragmatism A distinctly American philosophical movement that stressed practical and pragmatic conventions, structures and thought. John Dewey is one such representative.

Anhedonia Refers to a symptom of severe mental illness during which one has lost the ability to feel pleasure. It occurs in depression and also as a negative symptom in psychosis.

Appetition Is a Whiteheadian term that holds all members of organic existence have some degree of appetite or desire to become and seek satisfaction.

Atypical Anti-psychotic Refers to the newer class of anti-psychotic medications, such as Risperdal, Seroquel and Zyprexa. They are "atypical" because they do not carry the "typical" forms of side-effects that accompany first-generation medications. This class of drugs is also unique because they target multiple neurochemical systems, e.g., both dopamine and serotonin systems.

Avolition Is the experience of the inability to initiate activity. Avolition can occur as a symptom of depression or as a negative symptom in psychosis. It refers to a general loss of will, intent or motivation that results in inactivity or loss of desire.

Benzodiazipine Receptor Is a neuron that allows drugs from the benzodiazipine class to bind to itself that results in a decrease of symptoms of anxiety. Its discovery suggested that the brain has neurochemical systems itself that are designed to modulate the experience of anxiety.

Christ-hymn Refers first of all to the poetic song about Christ in the second chapter of Philippians used by the Apostle Paul. There are similar poetic songs in other New Testament epistles as well.

Christology/Christological A form of theological construction that has as its subject matter the doctrine of Christ, or what meaning(s) Christ has for Christians. There are many varied christologies or doctrines about Christ in the New Testament and in the thought of various theologians.

Chronic Normals A whimsical phrase coined by the psychologist Fred Freese, who himself suffers with schizophrenia. It is a play on words that implicitly critiques a tendency of providers to refer to persons with severe mental illness as being "chronically mentally ill."

Clinical Pastoral Education/CPE Is a type of theological education that occurs mostly in hospitals wherein students learn about themselves, illness and suffering from the patients themselves--the "living human documents." This mode of field education is used to train seminary students, pastors and hospital chaplains in the art of pastoral care and counseling.

Command Hallucination Is an audible hallucination during which one hears a "voice" commanding him/her to do something or perform a task. They can be as benign as being commanded to take a bath or walk the dog, or as sinister as being instructed to take one's own life or the life of another.

Consumer A person with severe mental illness who seeks and receives mental health treatment and services. It is largely a term of self-designation and of identification with others who need and obtain such treatment services.

Conversion Refers to the religious or spiritual process and experience of being persuaded by the divine to transition from a lesser degree to a higher degree of holy life and/or psychospiritual health.

DSM IV Stands for *The Diagnostic & Statistical Manual, IVth Edition*. This book's standards are used by providers to define and diagnose the symptoms and character of the mental illnesses.

Deconstruction A late 20th Century philosophical and literary movement that was largely initiated in the post-structuralist thought and writing of Frenchmen Michel Foucault and Jacques Derrida. My tendency in this book is to use Foucault's "archeology" of power structures to undercut and expose "hidden agendas" and unstated foundational presuppositions of the status quo.

De/constructive I use this phrase to designate my method of textual analysis and construction. This method is de/constructive because it simultaneously lays bare and exposes received textual bias while erecting or constructing new and/or alternative readings, meanings and interpretations.

Deinstitutionalization Refers to the exodus of consumers from the psychiatric hospitals to the "least restrictive environment" of treatment in their home communities. This movement began in the 1950's and continues to this day.

Delusion Is a false thought or belief held to be true by the sufferer. It is a symptom of psychosis where one is rigidly fixed on an idea that is factually untrue. Delusions can be grandiose, paranoid, persecutory, homicidal and/or suicidal. They are symptomatic expressions of psychopathology.

Delusions of Grandeur Are symptoms of psychosis during which one has an exaggerated or over-inflated sense of self. An example would be one's false belief that s/he is a billionaire who is earth's emperor.

Delusions of Persecution Are symptoms of psychosis during which one thinks and feels oneself to be victimized constantly by another person or group. An example would be the false belief that the CIA and General Motors have actively conspired to ensure that one cannot obtain employment.

Dopamine Is an important neurochemical involved in psychotic processes. Because too much dopamine contributes to increased symptoms of psychosis, anti-psychotic medications seek to decrease dopamine levels and thereby reduce or moderate symptoms of psychosis.

El Shaddai Frequently translated as "God Almighty," this Old Testament name for God is sometimes translated by feminist interpreters as "The Breasted One."

Emmanuel A New Testament word used in the Gospel of Matthew to name Jesus that means "God is with us."

Empathy Is the clinical and therapeutic ability to "feel with or for" another. As unqualified acceptance, empathy is the emotive bedrock on which therapeutic alliances are built that enable and sustain the healing of psychological wounds.

Family Systems Refers to a broad range of psychodynamic theories in which family stress is defined as the pathological precipitant of individual mental illness. Family system theories have tended to define families in a causal role that (supposedly) causes the mental illness of a child or family member.

Fusion of Horizons Gadamer used this phrase to express the moment of coming to truth or understanding that occurs when the identities of texts and/or persons merge or fuse to become a new, mutually informed and transformed horizon or continuum of meaning.

GABA System A neurochemical system that functions to moderate and reduce anxiety.

Hallucination Is a devastating symptom of psychotic illness. This cluster of symptoms involves gross perceptual anomalies caused by neuropathology. Hallucinations can be audible, where one hears "voices" or other sounds that do not correspond to reality; visual, where one sees things that do not really exist; and/or tactile, where ones senses, feels or smells things that are not real. When they occur the sufferer believes his/her experience to be real and accurate, although they are patently false and exist only in one's "broken brain."

Hermeneutics Is a term I define as the art of interpretation. Hermeneutics, or methods of interpretation, have long been of interest to theologians and interpreters of the Bible. As a modern concern, philosophical hermeneutics have focused on the event of understanding, following in large the trajectories of thought of Martin Heidegger and Hans Georg Gadamer. As the art of interpretation, hermeneutics can be used to define any interpretative scheme, method, diagnostic tool or treatment modality that seeks to understand texts--both human and written.

Horizon Based on Heidegger, this term is used to express a continuum of experience that provides boundaries within which human meaning and identity are formed--in and by human and written texts.

IDDT Integrated Dual Diagnosis Treatment is a cutting-edge, evidence-based practice that treats consumers with substance problems on the basis of stage-sensitive interventions that seek to "reduce harm" while meeting the consumer with empathic acceptance "where s/he is" in terms of the processes of recovery. IDDT is unique in terms of its integrated, simultaneous treatment of issues of mental illness and addictions.

Ideas of Reference Symptoms of psychosis during which one believes him/herself to be receiving (secret) messages through various media: newspapers, TV, radio, books, print, or magazines, etc. These sorts of symptoms can also involve the mistaken assumptions that outside events are self-relevant

Infanticide The homicidal act of taking the life of one's child.

Johannine The scriptural tradition that associates the Gospel of John, the Epistles of John, and the Book of Revelation with Jesus' disciple, John.

Magical Thinking A symptom of psychosis during which one believes oneself to possess great or superhuman powers that can cause great good or great harm. It can also involve psychotic processes during which loose associations or connections have overstated, fortuitous meaning and impact.

Malleus Malificarum Was the title of the book, *Hammer of Witches,* which was used for hundreds of years by Europeans to diagnose witchcraft. Modern students of psychology have disclosed that this book's diagnostic categories for witchcraft are parallel to modern definitions and diagnoses of mental illness.

Meaning Making The fundamental character of human being's abilities and capacities to interpret or make sense out of life while constructing reality.

Mnemonics Refers to the processes by which various traditions are remembered and portrayed by Scripture.

Mumbles A synonym for the "voices" or audible hallucinations some consumers hear that was coined by a client who used this term to identify her particular "voices."

NAMI National Alliance on Mental Illness. Comprised mostly by family members and a lesser number of consumers, NAMI is the nation's largest grassroots organization dedicated to advocacy regarding issues of mental illness. NAMI provides support, education, and advocacy at local, state, and national levels on behalf of families and persons touched by mental illness.

Narcissism In Freudian thought, this is a pathological feature of human self-absorption and pre-occupation. A narcissistic self is one that is concerned only with and animated by itself. However, for Heinz Kohut, there are elements of the personality that require healthy forms of narcissistic development to establish centered health. Narcissistic injury occurs when elements of the self are wounded that result in the negation, impairment and/or destruction of healthy self-image and self-interest. Narcissistic injury thus refers to the psychological damage suffered by the self that interferes with normal processes of the formation of healthy self-esteem and self-valuation.

Narrenschiff This German word is translated by Foucault as a "ship of fools." "Ships of Fools" in Europe confined persons with mental illness on these boats or ships that carried them until their death upon the high seas and/or major rivers.

Negative Symptoms Symptoms of psychosis or schizophrenia which are said to take away from or diminish one's abilities, such as avolition, anhedonia, alogia, or depression.

Neurobiology The scientific study of the brain's biological systems and structures.

Neurochemical Pathway Is a "circuit" of the brain through which chemical messages are sent back and forth between neurons, systems and structures by neurotransmitters that are chemical messengers. Untreated symptoms of severe mental illness can damage and impair the circuit's ability to function properly.

Neuroimaging Imaging techniques such as MRI, PET, and CT Scans are used by scientists to allow them to "see inside" the human brain as it performs its various tasks and functions. These techniques can establish baselines that image normal or healthy brains that can then be compared to brains diseased by mental illnesses.

Neuropathology The actual damage done to various of the brains' chemical and structural systems that results in symptoms of severe mental illness.

Neurotransmitter A "chemical messenger" that is used by the brain to send messages back and forth between neurons, neurochemical systems and brain structures. The suppression or over-excitation of certain of these chemicals result in symptoms of severe mental illness.

Norepinephrine A neurochemical transmitter that is involved in symptoms of depression and other mood problems. Low levels of this neurochemical lead to depression, such that increases in its brain levels can help reduce and moderate depressive symptoms.

Paranoia A symptom of psychosis during which one experiences unrelenting, irrational fear. This type of delusion can involve complex systems of irrational thinking during which the sufferer believes and feels his/her safety and well being are threatened or placed in jeopardy. An example could be one of thinking the CIA has implanted computer chips in one's brain to track and monitor one's activities and movements, while reading one's mind to impede and thwart one's desires. Essentially, paranoia is an unwarranted suspicion that others are out to get you.

Patriarch   A male tribal or cultic leader whose life is regarded as a paradigm of behavior for others to emulate or follow.

Pharmacology   The scientific research, study and development of medicinal interventions.

Positive Symptoms   Symptoms of psychosis or schizophrenia that add pathological characteristics to the sufferer, such as hallucinations or delusions.

Process Philosophy   A 20th Century philosophical movement that is based largely on the thought of Alfred North Whitehead and that of Charles Hartshorne. Process philosophy asserts that all of reality is in a process of becoming, flux, and creative advance, as opposed to static being.

Process Theology   A 20th Century, largely Protestant and North American movement of philosophical theology based on the tenets of process philosophy. Among its leaders are John Cobb, Schubert Ogden, William Beardslee, Daniel Day Williams, and Marjorie Suchockie. Process theology seeks to address how God, nature and humanity relate in concert and mutual exchange to advance creatively the beauty and satisfaction of all reality.

Provider   A mental health professional who provides treatment services to consumers.

Psychopathology   Refers to the symptoms, deficits and impairments associated with the experience of severe mental illness.

Psychopharmacology   The scientific research, study and development of specifically psychiatric medicines.

Psychosis   Refers to the cluster of symptoms that define the thought disorders. These can include hallucinations and or delusions, and the so-called negative symptoms. One is said to be "psychotic" when one experiences such symptoms.

Psychospiritual Is the realm of experience where the psyche/soul interacts with the spirit. The psyche and spirit interact as polar elements within human being's relation to God and the world that enable the formation of meaning in life.

Psychospiritual Hermeneutics The field or art of interpretative endeavor that seeks to uncover and disclose the essential unity of psyche and spirit in texts--both human and written.

Receptor The part of a neuron that receives or allows a neurotransmitter to bind to it.

Recovery Borrowed from the 12-Step traditions, this word is used by some consumers to designate their initial and sustained commitment to treatment and optimum personal mental health.

Severe Mental Illness Refers to the broad spectrum of diagnoses and experiences of anxiety, depression, bipolar illness, and schizophrenia.

SSRI Selective Serotonin Re-Uptake Inhibitor. A modern class of anti-depressant medications whose action prohibits the re-absorption of serotonin and thereby decreases symptoms of depression by increasing available levels of serotonin within the brain. Prozac was the first medicine in this class of drugs that also includes Zoloft and Lexapro, for example.

Self Object Heinz Kohut designated this phrase to describe how an empathic caregiver becomes the therapeutic ally and object in and through which a wounded self can script his/her healing.

Serotonin Is a neurochemcial that leads to depression when its levels in the brain are too low. Increased levels of serotonin within the brain can decrease symptoms of depression and other mood problems.

Shaman Is a traditional healer such as a "medicine man" or "witch doctor" who seeks altered states of consciousness (similar to symptoms of mental illness) in order to perform his/her tasks and arts of healing.

Solidarity In this book solidarity refers to the clinical and theological relatedness in which God and persons provide pragmatic support and empathy.

Stigma The social blame and shame connected to the experience of severe mental illness. (Stigma is not limited to mental illness, but applies equally as well to other "socially unacceptable" diseases, e.g., HIV/AIDS, leprosy and others.)

Synoptic Gospels Matthew, Mark and Luke are known by this term because when they are placed in parallel their written texts are shown to be highly similar.

Theodicy The theological dilemma how to reconcile claims and definitions that God is all-loving and all-powerful given the reality of genuine evil. As logic would have it, the reality of genuine evil prevents God from being both all-powerful and all-loving as classically defined.

Thought Disorder Refers to the diagnoses of schizophrenia and psychoses that primarily involve symptoms of irregular and anomalous thought and/or thought's expression.

Typical Anti-psychotic One of several first-generation anti-psychotic medications, such as thorazine, stellazine or haldol, that carry a unique set of physiological side-effects that can include uncontrollable muscle stiffness, tremors, somatic restlessness, and/or facial spasms or tongue "darting." They are also typical in the restrictive sense that they tend to moderate only levels of dopamine in the brain.

Unclean Refers to a host of foods, diseases, persons and/or locations or places that would make a Hebrew or Jew religiously impure or defiled.

Unconcealment How the German philosopher Martin Heidegger defined truth. The event of unconcealment is one wherein the concealed becomes made known, wherein the hidden is brought to light and exposed, wherein the obscure is made clear, or wherein truth is revealed or disclosed.

Will to Power Nietzsche's fascination with the individual's ability to rise above and assert itself and its will beyond the narrow confines and conventions of the "herd" mentality. It includes the self's desire to dominate, subordinate and create reality.

APPENDIX
The Facts about Mental Illness

- At any given time, 50 million Americans suffer from a mental disorder (Surgeon General's Report, 1999; "SGR")

- In 1996, the United States spent $99 billion for the direct treatment of mental illnesses, substance abuse and Alzheimer's (SGR 1999)

- In 1990 (the most recent year for this statistic), the United States' economy lost $79 billion in productivity costs, of which: $63 billion were lost in productivity; $12 billion were lost in productivity due to premature deaths associated with mental illnesses; and $4 billion were lost to incarcerations, and burdens imposed on families who provide direct care (SGR, 1999).

- In 1990 (most recent statistic), a breakdown of the global burden of economic losses due to mental illnesses in countries with established market economies reveals that 15.4% of all health/illness-related economic losses were due solely to mental illnesses, which was second only to the 18.6% of all cardiovascular conditions (SGR, 1999)

- In 1993, 26% of all SSDI payments were made to persons disabled by mental illnesses (NAMI.org, 2000)

- In 1993, 28.1% of all SSI payments were made to persons disabled by mental illnesses (NAMI.org, 2000)

- 25% of all hospital beds in the United States are occupied by psychiatrically ill patients, which are more beds than all the victims of heart disease, cancer and respiratory ailments combined (NARSAD, 1999)

- 17% - 20% of all Americans will suffer a depressive episode during their lifetime (NARSAD, 1999)

- Roughly 1% of all populations will suffer with schizophrenia (NAMI Indiana, 2005)

- Roughly 2% of all populations will suffer with bipolar illness (NAMI Indiana, 2005)

- 35% of all homeless Americans are estimated to be suffering from (usually untreated) mental illnesses (NARSAD, 1999)

- The Federal Government of the United States spends $10 on research per person with depression; and $14 per person with schizophrenia (Compared to Federal research funding spent at the rate of: $161 per patient with multiple sclerosis; $1,000 per patient with muscular dystrophy; $130 per patient with heart disease; and $203 per patient with cancer--NARSAD, 1999)

Bibliography

Allness, Deborah J., and Knoedler, William H. The PACT Model. Arlington, VA: Programs of Assertive Community Treatment, Inc. 1998.

Andreasen, Nancy C. Brave New Brain: Conquering Mental Illness in the Age of the Genome. New York: Oxford University Press. 2001.

_____ The Broken Brain. New York: Harper & Row, Publishers. 1985.

Asquith, Glenn H., Editor. Vision from a Little Known Country. Journal of Pastoral Care Publications, Inc. 1992.

Bishop, Marilyn, Editor. Religion and Disability. Kansas City: Sheed & Ward. 1995.

Boisen, Anton. Out of the Depths. New York: Harper & Row, Publishers. 1960.

Brown, Delwin. To Set at Liberty. Maryknoll, NY: Orbis Books. 1981.

Fawcett, Jan; Golden, Bernard; & Rosenfeld, Nancy. New Hope for People with Bipolar Disorder. New York, New York: Three Rivers Press. 2000.

Foucault, Michel. <u>The Archeology of Knowledge.</u> New York: Pantheon Books. 1972.

_____ <u>Madness and Civilization.</u> New York: Vintage Books. 1965.

_____ <u>Power/Knowledge.</u> New York: Pantheon Books. 1977.

Fowler, James. <u>Stages of Faith.</u> San Francisco: Harper. 1981.

Frankl, Viktor E. <u>Man's Search for Meaning.</u> New York, NY: Washington Square Press Publications. 1984.

Gadamer, Hans-Georg. <u>Truth and Method.</u> New York: The Crossroad Publishing Co. 1984.

Gerkin, Charles V. <u>The Living Human Document.</u> Nashville: Abingdon Press. 1984.

Heidegger, Martin. <u>Being and Time.</u> San Francisco: Harper & Row, Publishers, Incorporated. 1962.

Jamison, Kay Redfield. <u>An Unquiet Mind.</u> New York: Vintage Books. 1995.

Kohut, Heinz. <u>Self Psychology and the Humanities.</u> New York: W.W. Norton & Company. 1985.

Krell, David Farrell. <u>Martin Heidegger: Basic Writings.</u> New York: Harper & Row, Publishers. 1977.

Nietzsche, Friedrich. <u>The Will to Power.</u> New York: Vintage Books. 1967.

Nouwen, Henri J. M. <u>The Wounded Healer.</u> Garden City, New York: Doubleday & Company, Inc. 1979.

Novalis, Peter N., Rojcewicz, Stephen J., Jr., Peele, Roger. <u>Clinical

<u>Manual of Supportive Psychotherapy.</u> Washington, DC: American Psychiatric Press, Inc. 1993.

Randall, Robert L. <u>Pastor and Parish.</u> New York, NY: Human Sciences Press, Inc. 1988.

Rogers, Carl. <u>Client-Centered Therapy.</u> Boston: Houghton Mifflin Company. 1951.

Ross, J. F. "Wine," pp. 849-852. <u>The Interpreter's Dictionary of the Bible, Vol. 4.</u> Nashville: Abingdon Press. 1962.

Schweizer, Eduard. <u>The Good News According to Mark.</u> Atlanta: John Knox Press. 1970.

Whitehead, Alfred North. <u>Process and Reality.</u> New York: The Free Press. 1978.

Williamson, Jr., Lamar. <u>Mark.</u> Louisville: John Knox Press. 1983.

<u>The Spiritual Formation Bible.</u> New Revised Standard Version. Grand Rapids, Michigan: Zondervan Publishing House. 1999.

Printed in the United States
56710LVS00006B/151-174

9 781425 900090